EDITED BY **KAREN WESPIESER**
SERIES EDITOR **TOM BENNETT**

THE research **ED** GUIDE TO

SPECIAL EDUCATIONAL NEEDS

AN EVIDENCE-INFORMED
GUIDE FOR TEACHERS

First Published 2021

by John Catt Educational Ltd,
15 Riduna Park, Station Road,
Melton, Woodbridge IP12 1QT

Tel: +44 (0) 1394 389850
Email: enquiries@johncatt.com
Website: www.johncatt.com

ISBN: 978 1 912906 40 6

Set and designed by John Catt Educational Limited

WHAT IS researchED?

researchED is an international, grassroots education-improvement movement that was founded in 2013 by Tom Bennett, a London-based high school teacher and author. researchED is a truly unique, teacher-led phenomenon, bringing people from all areas of education together onto a level playing field. Speakers include teachers, principals, professors, researchers and policy makers.

Since our first sell-out event, researchED has spread all across the UK, into the Netherlands, Norway, Sweden, Australia, the USA, with events planned in Spain, Japan, South Africa and more. We hold general days as well as themed events, such as researchED Maths & Science, or researchED Tech.

WHO ARE WE?

Since 2013, researchED has grown from a tweet to an international conference movement that so far has spanned six continents and thirteen countries. We have simple aims: to help teaching become more evidence-facing; to raise the research literacy in teaching; to improve education research standards; and to bring research users and research creators closer together. To do this, we hold unique one-day conferences that bring together teachers, researchers, academics and anyone touched by research. We believe in teacher voice, and short-circuiting the top-down approach to education that benefits no one.

HOW DOES IT WORK?

The gathering of mainly teachers, researchers, school leaders, policymakers and edu-bloggers creates a unique dynamic. Teachers and researchers can attend the sessions all day and engage with each other to exchange ideas. The vast majority of speakers stay for the duration of the conference, visit each other's sessions, work on the expansion of their knowledge and gain a deeper understanding of the work of their peers. Teachers can take note of recent developments in educational research, but are also given the opportunity to provide feedback on the applicability of research or practical obstacles.

CONTENTS

FOREWORD
BY TOM BENNETT

As a rookie teacher 100 years ago, I was immediately struck by the breadth of demand in the comprehensive classroom. Some students tore into every task almost before I'd set them; some struggled to begin and teared up at the thought of completing them; some barely tried, or tore up the books instead. To the beginner, it's easy to attribute every behaviour or misbehaviour to the student's intentions and imagine that everything a student does is done because they have deliberately, rationally and carefully chosen to do so. It's easy to fall into this mistake.

But mistake it was. In my very first lesson I learned a lesson of my own; some students performed and behaved the way they did because they enjoyed the advantages of circumstance and were free to make the choices they did. Some struggled with impediments that weighed heavily on their actions, such as stress, abuse, bullying, mental health issues and more. They wrestled with burdens that tipped the scales of their choices, and in ways that those more fortunate could barely guess. And then there were students who coped – or sometimes didn't – with circumstances that reduced or limited their choices, such as neurological impairments. It was clear that the image of the perfectly free, rational actor in the classroom, was often a myth.

And every teacher must remember this. We do not sign up to teach only some children, or children that are easy to teach. If this is your ambition, comprehensive or state sector education is likely not your best path. But if you are dedicated to teaching children in all of their moments, and through all circumstances whether they be carefree or challenging, then you will find the role of a teacher one of the most satisfying in the world. All children, whatever their beginnings, are capable of going further, and helping to make that happen is an honour and a great responsibility.

But often the most disadvantaged students suffer from a disadvantage that also can affect all students: teaching strategies that are not evidence-informed. This is a problem throughout the estate of education, and prompted the creation of researchED itself. But the sleep of reason produces monsters, and when we surrender our practice to hunches and instinct and voodoo and folk teaching, well… We might get lucky and find that the strategies work. Or we might not. But what we won't know is why something helped and how we can replicate or improve that success. Teaching is not a hard science, but it is also not purely an art form. When we teach in ways that merely appeal to us rather than because we have strong reasons to believe they are suitable and efficient, then we practise a disservice on the students, who expect and deserve better.

And when we do so with students who are already disadvantaged, then we doubly disadvantage them. We can do much better. As this book beautifully curated by Karen Wespieser shows, the field of education for children with special educational needs is broad and complex, and in places suffers from a deficit of research bases. At times it leans, like many other areas of education, heavily into fancy, snake oil psychology and fiction. But sometimes it provides us with enormously useful strategies that we can use in individual circumstances as well as more universal ones. It supports us by helping our practice to be evidence-informed rather than evidence-based, and that makes all the difference. Especially to those of our learners who need it the most. We need to celebrate our burgeoning understanding of what processes help children with complex or challenging needs, and embrace with enthusiasm the conversations about evidence, scientific enquiry, and the fruits of our emergent understandings. Never before has it been more important to not simply ask 'What works?' but 'When do things work, and when do they not? And by how much? And to what end? And at what cost? And with whom?' I never said this was going to be easy. But I can tell you that it is entirely worth it.

Tom Bennett

Founder, researchED

Series editor

INTRODUCTION

What this book covers (and what it doesn't)

It was an honour to be invited to compile and edit the researchED book on SEND, but as always with these types of projects there was a worry in the back of my mind that it could be a poisoned chalice.

Although I have worked in the SEND education sector, I would not call myself an expert in SEND. I do know a thing or two about research and evidence though so aimed to pin this book on that expertise instead.

A book on SEND can be arranged in many ways and could include a multitude of topics. As many of the contributors to the book argue, SEND is often a very personal topic and can be deeply rooted in individual cases. It can therefore be difficult to draw common themes both from research and from experience.

As a starting point I wanted to avoid talking in too much depth about individual conditions – it is likely that in your class you have a learner with literacy difficulties, a learner with an autistic spectrum disorder, a learner with mental health challenges. For these cases and for others that you will come across in your teaching career, I suggest that you look at the specialist literature. One chapter in a general SEND book is not going to be enough to help you support your learner, so we haven't tried.

Instead, I reverted to a slightly dated – but still widely considered useful – way of thinking about SEND to organise the book. The 'wave' approach takes you through universal provision (what every teacher should be doing in every classroom for those with SEND and it will probably work well for those without too; targeted provision (still within mainstream schools, but encompassing specific pedagogies or interventions); and specialist provision (provided by specialist staff or specialist schools).

Alternatively, the book can also be read according to the evidence base that underpins each chapter as depicted in the table below.

Quantitative SEND data	Chapter 1	How many learners with SEND are there?
	Chapter 5	Maximising the role, contribution and impact of teaching assistants
	Chapter 11	Alternative provision and SEND
Literature and meta-studies on SEND	Chapter 2	Putting research evidence to work in SEND
	Chapter 3	What is inclusive teaching and how do you know if you're doing it?
	Chapter 7	No SENCO is an island
	Chapter 10	Single, separate and surprising souls: the past, present and future role of research in SEND
Collecting, sharing and using SEND data	Chapter 4	Dual coding: the big wins for learners with SEND
	Chapter 6	One-page profiles: creating your own evidence
	Chapter 8	SEND in practice
	Chapter 9	Evidence-informed special schools: do we have enough evidence?

SEND is also, to an extent, a cultural phenomenon. The very terminology is different even within the four countries of the UK (for example SEND is referred to as Additional Support for Learning in Scotland). It is for this reason that – despite researchED being an international movement – this book focuses on England, certainly regarding national statistics (chapter 1 and chapter 11). Chapters about collecting, sharing and using SEND data with a wider range of evidence or experience will hopefully be of more use in a wider range of contexts.

The evidence base

If much of the evidence base in education is still half-baked, the evidence base in SEND is raw. Despite the medical nature of some SEND there is limited robust evidence on how best to support these learners educationally. As Barney Angliss explains in chapter 10, few trials include learners with SEND or special schools and the Education Endowment Foundation (EEF) have only just begun their first set of SEND-focused work.

Because of this, compiling this book was perhaps not as easy as some of the others in the researchED series. Evidence-informed approaches do not seem as prevalent among SEND practitioners; whether this is a cause or effect of the sparsity of evidence cannot be known.

Despite this, all the authors in this book have endeavoured to evidence their arguments and provide a clear research base for their approaches. You will notice however, a number of sources being repeatedly referenced, highlighting the sparsity of good-quality evidence in this field of education. I hope this book will begin to change this.

Common themes

Across the 11 chapters of this book, three themes in particular seem to keep occurring: high-quality teaching, the importance of the appropriate deployment of teaching assistants to support learners with SEND, and the need for clear communication and partnership with the parents of learners with SEND.

'High-quality' teaching

The importance of 'high-quality' teaching as the first response when supporting children and young people with SEND is underlined in the SEND Code of Practice (DfE, 2015), and features in a number of chapters of the book. For example, it is one of the eight areas investigated by Cullen et al. for the EEF Evidence Review that I recommend as essential reading in my overview of SEND evidence in chapter 2. Yet its frequent use does not mean that it's an uncontested term. In chapter 7, Nicole Dempsey provides this succinct definition of high-quality teaching:

> *We know what a high-quality education looks like too because we do it every day for our learners who are not identified as SEND.*

Katherine Walsh meanwhile dedicates much of chapter 3 to exploring what the term means in practice. She emphasises that teachers should adapt their teaching before considering pull-out interventions and reminds us of evidence that learners' attainment is 'strongly affected by the quantity and pacing of instruction'. Ultimately, Katherine recommends careful planning of lessons to ensure all children and young people have the opportunity to learn.

Similar approaches are recommended by Cassie Young in chapter 8 as she traces back the roots of high-quality teaching to 'quality first teaching' and the National Strategies.

Teaching assistants

The evidence base around the deployment of teaching assistants (TAs) is explored in detail by Rob Webster and Matthew Parker in chapter 5, but their role in supporting learners with SEND is also picked up in chapter 2 in relation to training in interventions and in EEF review and guidance documents, in chapter 3 as part of a discussion of inclusive teaching, and in chapter 8 in real-life examples of deployment based on learner need.

Webster and Parker refer to TAs as 'the currency of SEND provision'. It is hard to tell whether their frequent citation in this book is due to this bedrock position in the SEND landscape, or because it is one of the main areas, related to SEND, where there is a systematic evidence base. Either way, it is clear that they have an important role to play and it is crucial that SEND practitioners have a clear understanding of the evidence on how best to deploy them.

Parents

The EEF (2021) state that 'parents play a crucial role in supporting their children's learning, and levels of parental engagement are consistently associated with better academic outcomes.' Yet there is surprisingly little robust evidence on which approaches are most effective in improving parental engagement (Turner, 2018). However, as a common theme in this book, it appears that it is a strong hypothesis that this is even more important when it comes to SEND. Indeed, in his re-imagining of SEND research (chapter 10), Barney Angliss makes a strong case for greater inclusion of parental data within education research itself.

The role of parental engagement comes through in a number of other chapters too: Kenny Wheeler devotes an entire section to the role of parents in chapter 6 explaining the importance of engaging with parents as part of collecting holistic data on a young person's life. In chapter 8, Cassie Young provides examples of the importance of structured conversations with parents and in chapter 9, Sabrina Hobbs gives worked examples of parental engagement in her special school setting.

As with the evidence base around TAs, it's hard to make a call on the direction of causality of this theme. But as an intervention that is frequently at low or no cost, it is certainly an area that ought to be within the research-informed playbook of every SEND practitioner.

A note on language

The language of SEND can be tricky; there are a lot of acronyms and a constant fear that you might not be being politically correct. One of the initial problems that you hit when writing about special educational needs is when and where you include 'disability'. SEN or SEND? For the sake of simplicity, I have taken the editorial decision to refer to SEND throughout except when writing about SEN Support (as that has a specific meaning of its own). For an editor, consistency is king, so that is the term used in each chapter of this book.

Where there is no specific reference to a phase of education, we have used the term 'learner' rather than student or pupil as this is a more generic term that applies to all areas of education. Again, this is primarily for consistency.

Finally, I have not asked contributors to spell out every abbreviation as (I hope) you will be reading the book as a whole! Instead, you can find a glossary of the abbreviations used at the end of this book.

References

Department for Education. (2015) *Special educational needs and disability code of practice: 0 to 25 years.* London: DfE.

EEF. (2021) *Working with Parents to Support Children's Learning.* Available at: https://educationendowmentfoundation.org.uk/education-evidence/ guidance-reports/supporting-parents (Accessed 28 September 2021).

Turner, J. (2018) *EEF Blog: The hard lessons of parental engagement.* Available at: https://educationendowmentfoundation.org.uk/news/eef-blog-the-hard-lessons-of-parental-engagement (Accessed 28 September 2021).

PART 1
THE BIG PICTURE

This section sets the scene of SEND education in England. Richard Selfridge looks at the number of learners with SEND in England and trends over time and Karen Wespieser provides an overview of the evidence base introducing some of the key meta-studies and guiding the reader in the basics of evidence-informed SEND practice.

1. HOW MANY LEARNERS WITH SEND ARE THERE?

RICHARD SELFRIDGE

Teacher, researcher and self-confessed data geek Richard Selfridge looks at the big picture of SEND provision in England. Using a rich DfE dataset, Richard helps put into context the changing SEND need in the education system.

As is frequently noted, every teacher is a teacher of SEND, and Richard's reminder that nine out of 10 learners with SEND are in mainstream schools makes clear why this maxim is so important. However, Richard's analysis also highlights how the primary area of need of learners with SEND varies by phase and school type; understanding this may help teachers prioritise and recognise the educational needs they may most likely be called upon to support.

The DfE's annual collection and publication of data about learners with SEND is a great source of information about how many learners have SEND, what type of school they attend and what their primary area of need is. Using this data, we can track changes over time and investigate trends in SEND and SEND provision.

The Special Educational Needs (SEN) Information Act (2008)

Since 2009, the UK government has published statutory data detailing the number of children within the English school system known to have special educational needs and disabilities above and beyond their peers. The SEN Information Act (2008) requires the Secretary of State to publish information about children in England with special educational needs to help improve the wellbeing of these children. The first data was published in 2009, and annual data is released each July.

The data is collected each January as part of the annual school census. Headteachers or SENCOs are asked how many learners in their school have SEND and to record the 'primary area of need'. This means that while the number of learners with SEND are recorded with a relatively high degree of accuracy, the need of the learner may not be, as issues such as comorbidity and accuracy of assessment are not taken into account.

The data covers special schools in both the state and independent sectors: state-funded mainstream nursery, primary and secondary schools, as well as pupil referral units (PRUs) and schools in the independent (non-government funded) sector. The data includes children aged from 0 to 17, with a small number of children aged 18 (0.25% of the school population) and 19+ (0.006% of the school population).

Since 2015, children have been classified as either having an Education, Health and Care Plan (EHCP) or requiring SEN Support. EHCPs are awarded by Local Authorities (LAs) if a child is deemed to need more support than is available through SEN Support. SEN Support is provided within a school setting and is provided by the school.

How many learners with SEND are there in England?

In January 2020 there were 1.37 million learners with SEND in England's schools. These children represented just under one in six (15.5%) of the school learner population. There were 294,800 learners (3.3%) with EHCPs for children deemed to need more support than is available through SEN Support in schools, and 1,079,000 learners (12.1%) receiving SEN Support (additional support for children with special educational needs but without EHCPs) in schools.

The majority of learners with SEND are educated in mainstream schools in England

In total nine out of 10 learners with SEND are educated in mainstream schools, although this falls to 55.3% of learners with EHCPs. 9.5% of learners with an identified SEND were educated in special schools for learners with SEND. Special schools cater primarily for those with autism spectrum disorders (684 schools), severe learning difficulty (561 schools) and moderate learning difficulty (537). Schools may be approved for more than one type of provision.

Just under half (44.7%) of learners with EHCPs and 1.1% of learners receiving SEN Support were being educated in special schools in 2020. 1% of learners with SEND were educated in PRUs although those with SEND make up 81% of all learners in PRUs. Around one in 14 (7.1%/98,079) learners with SEND are educated in the independent sector.

The percentage of children with EHCPs is beginning to rise

In each year from 2007 to 2017 the number of learners with EHCPs (or Statements of special educational needs prior to 2015) represented 2.8% of the school population. 2018 saw a small increase, with 2.9% of learners having EHCPs. 2019 saw a further increase, with 3.1% of learners having EHCPs. In 2020, 3.3% of learners had EHCPs.

It should be noted that, unlike the surprisingly static percentage of children in England with EHCPs in the 10 years to 2017, the school population was more volatile, growing 11% between 2009 and 2018 (from 8,092,280 to 8,890,345).

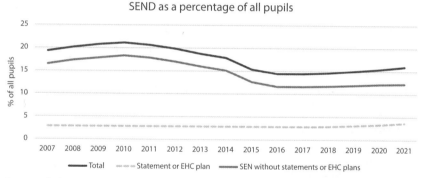

Source: DfE (2021) Special educational needs in England and DfE (2018) Special educational needs in England: January 2018.

But the number of children classified as needing SEN Support has varied over time

The fluctuations in SEN Support (School Action and School Action Plus prior to 2015) are clearly much greater than those for children with EHCPs. The mean number of children in this category was 1,483,453 between 2007 and 2019. The peak year – 2010 – saw almost 500,000 more children in the SEN Support category than at the low point of 2016 (despite there being 450,000 more children in the school system in 2016 compared to 2010).

Primary areas of SEND need in the English school system

Learners with SEND are classified by their primary area of need. There are four broad areas of need in the SEND Code of Practice:

1. Communication and interaction.
2. Cognition and learning.
3. Social, emotional and mental health.
4. Sensory and/or physical needs (DfE, 2015).

Summaries of areas of need	
Communication and interaction	**Social, emotional and mental health (SEMH)**
Speech, language and communications needs (SLCN) – where learners have difficulty communicating with others Autistic spectrum disorder (ASD) – where learners are likely to have difficulty with social interaction	A broad category where learners may experience a wide range of social and emotional difficulties, including disorders such as attention deficit disorder or attachment disorder
Cognition and learning	**Sensory and/or physical needs**
Moderate learning difficulty (MLD) – where children learn at a slower rate than their peers Severe learning difficulty (SLD) – where cognition difficulties are compounded by associated difficulties with mobility and communication Profound and multiple learning difficulty (PMLD) – where learners are likely to have severe and complex learning difficulties, often in addition to physical disability or sensory impairment Specific learning difficulty (SpLD) – where learners are affected by one or more specific aspects of learning such as dyslexia (reading and writing difficulties), dyscalculia (numerical difficulties) and dyspraxia (movement difficulties)	Hearing impairment Visual impairment Multi-sensory impairment – where learners have a combination of vision and hearing difficulties Physical disability – where learners require additional ongoing support and equipment to access education

Any children who do not fit into the four broad categories may have SEND categorised separately as 'other difficulty/disability'.

Changes by age, phase and school type

The percentage of children with EHCPs increases as learners progress through school. In particular, there are noticeable changes over time as children approach secondary school age, with steady increases through primary before a levelling off in secondary.

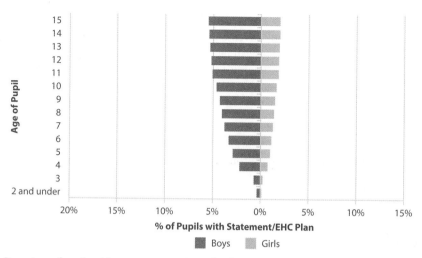

Percentage of pupils with a statement or EHC plan by age and gender in state-funded primary, secondary and special schools, England (2018). Source: DfE (2018) Special educational needs in England: January 2018.

The primary areas of need also change as learners move through the education system. For example, while SLCN is the largest area of need in primary schools this does not feature in the top three areas of SEN Support in secondary schools (it appears fourth, with 47,574 learners in the category in 2018). The number of learners recorded within this category reduces each year as children progress through the school system, as can be seen below.

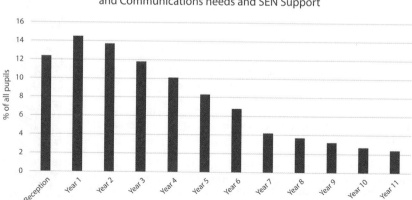

Source: DfE (2021) Special educational needs in England.

In conclusion

While there has been a recent increase in the percentage of learners with EHCPs in England's schools, the long-term picture has been consistent over time, with close to one in 30 children having high needs. In addition, one in every 10 learners has special educational needs or disabilities which require additional support over and above that which is provided for all children in the school system.

Within the overall category of SEND, there are large groups of learners with common needs and smaller groups of children requiring highly specific support. The picture changes over the course of the statutory education age range, with different needs both being met and becoming apparent as learners progress through school.

References and further reading

DfE. (2015) *Special educational needs and disability code of practice: 0 to 25 years*. London: DfE.

DfE. (2018) Special educational needs in England: January 2018. Available at: https://assets.publishing.service.gov.uk/government/uploads/system/ uploads/attachment_data/file/729208/SEN_2018_Text.pdf (Accessed: 18 October 2021).

DfE. (2019) *Children with special educational needs and disabilities (SEND)*. Available at: https://www.gov.uk/children-with-special-educational-needs/ extra-SEN-help. (Accessed: 21 April 2021).

DfE. (2021) *Special educational needs in England*. Available at: https:// explore-education-statistics.service.gov.uk/find-statistics/special- educational-needs-in-england (Accessed: 21 April 2021).

DfE/DoH. (2015) *Special educational needs and disability code of practice: 0 to 25 years*. Available at: https://assets.publishing.service.gov.uk/ government/uploads/system/uploads/attachment_data/file/398815/SEND_ Code_of_Practice_January_2015.pdf (Accessed: 21 April 2021).

NASEN. (2015) *The SEND Code of Practice: 0 to 25 years*. Available at: https://nasen.org.uk/resources/send-code-practice-0-25-years (Accessed: 21 April 2021).

Ofsted. (2018) *Ofsted Annual Report 2017-18*. Available at: https://assets.publishing.service.gov.uk/government/uploads/system/ uploads/attachment_data/file/761606/29523_Ofsted_Annual_ Report_2017-18_041218.pdf (Accessed 21 April 2021).

2. PUTTING RESEARCH EVIDENCE TO WORK IN SEND

KAREN WESPIESER

Karen Wespieser is an education researcher with over 20 years' experience of applied research. Recent roles have included directing operations at a charity for SEND and establishing the SEND curriculum for the Oak National Academy. In 2020 Karen was awarded an MBE for services to children with special educational needs. Using this experience, Karen considers some of the best available evidence on SEND and recommends how to go about applying it in different settings.

Unsurprisingly, the list of recommended research that focuses on SEND is short. But synthesis, and in particular the EEF Guidance Report, and the EEF-style evidence guide tables produced by Ask Research and Coventry University, should be on the bookshelf for all practitioners.

Being research-informed is an approach and a practitioner mindset; in many ways it oughtn't matter if you are currently supporting learners with SEND or not. However, we must always focus on the context of previous research in order to fully consider what might work in our own contexts.

As a busy practitioner, you must be selective in what research evidence you will read

A good way of making the most of the scarce amount of time you have available for reading is to try and find authoritative summaries of research evidence. Below is a short summary of three such studies.

Special Educational Needs in mainstream schools: Evidence review by Cullen et al. 2020

Mairi Ann Cullen and colleagues from the Centre for Educational Development, Appraisal and Research (CEDAR) at University of Warwick were commissioned by the EEF to inform the SEND Guidance document (EEF, 2020). The review was commissioned explicitly as a broad overview of evidence across a range of topics, with the intention that the EEF might then commission further, more detailed reviews of specific areas within the broad SEND field. It was conducted in a systematic manner, but it was not commissioned as a systematic review. However, it prioritises evidence drawn from systematic reviews.

The study looks at eight areas:

- Evidence on inclusion
- Evidence on effective school leadership of SEND
- Evidence on assessment and identification of learning needs
- Evidence on high-quality teaching for pupils with SEND
- Evidence on using targeted interventions effectively
- Evidence on effective use of TAs and support staff re pupils with SEND
- Evidence on effective work with external support
- Evidence on schools' effective engagement of parents of pupils with SEND.

Cullen et al. conclude that overall, the strongest evidence relates to the impact on learner outcomes of everyday teaching practices occurring within the classroom (the microsystem). While the evidence related to the relationships school staff make with a learner's parents and relevant external professionals (the mesosystem) is reported as being 'highly relevant to England's mainstream schools', Cullen et al. report that the strength of evidence is medium at best. Similarly, evidence related to the decisions and practices of school leadership around SEND (the exosystem) is noted as being limited.

The subsequent guidance report uses the evidence to make five recommendations:

1. Create a positive and supportive environment for all learners without exception.
2. Build an ongoing, holistic understanding of your learners and their needs.
3. Ensure all learners have access to high-quality teaching.
4. Complement high-quality teaching with carefully selected small-group and one-to-one interventions.

5. Work effectively with teaching assistants.

SEN Support: A rapid evidence assessment by Carroll et al. 2017

Julia Carroll and her team at Coventry University were commissioned by the DfE to review what effective practice in school and post-16 institutions looks like and to develop understanding of how to improve outcomes for children and young people on SEN Support. They looked at SEN Support for children who had been identified with SEND and who required different or additional support to meet these needs, but who did not have a Statement of SEN or an EHCP.

In this rapid evidence assessment – which involved a more structured and rigorous search of the literature than a traditional literature review, though was not as comprehensive as a systematic review – Carroll et al. looked at 1046 studies carried out on young people aged between 4 and 19, published between 2000 and 2016. Following the application of a range of eligibility criteria, 541 studies were included in the final evidence assessment, resulting in a number of key findings.

Carroll et al. found a range of good-quality evidence about effective interventions in cognition, social, emotional and mental health (SEMH) and communication and interaction. On the other hand, the evidence about the teaching and adaptations that can support these needs is not as comprehensive.

The evidence assessment found that training in the use of an intervention has an important role to play in its effectiveness. Teaching professionals who are not trained in an intervention and who do not understand its principles will have less impact using an intervention than teaching assistants who have been appropriately trained in the use of the intervention.

It was also found that, regardless of the intervention, detailed assessment of the needs of each individual child is essential when trying to establish which approach to adopt, and that it cannot be assumed that training to remediate a particular weakness will automatically improve the target academic skill. It should therefore not be taken for granted that 'skills' will transfer from one use to another, for example, the development of memory skills will not necessarily improve learning.

Furthermore, Carroll et al. go on to note several gaps in the evidence base which include:

- The research evidence for supporting physical and sensory needs is much less extensive than for the other three areas of need and is often based on small-scale case studies.

- Most existing high-quality research is based on work in primary schools; there is much less research carried out in secondary schools and colleges.

- Most research studies provide a comparison between a particular approach and a 'no-treatment' control; this makes it very difficult to know which of two different approaches is likely to be more effective.

- Very little research examines individual differences in responsiveness to interventions; while all teachers know that certain approaches work better for some children than others, there is very little evidence as to why this occurs.

SEN Support: research evidence on effective approaches and examples of current practice in good and outstanding schools and colleges by Ask Research and Coventry University (2017a and 2017b)

Ask Research and Coventry University (2017a and 2017b) created a guidance document of both current good practice found in schools and colleges with suggestions for strategies to be adopted by school and college leaders. Of particular use are the summary tables which identify different approaches and strategies which appear to work in different key stages; whether the strategy is best suited for whole classes, small groups or individuals; the strength of the evidence; and where that evidence can be found.

The evidence base in communication and interaction approaches

Suitable for Key Stage 1/2 **P**

Strategy	Suitable for:	What is the strategy?	How strong is the evidence?	Where can I find out more?
Oral language intervention		A scripted language intervention led by teaching assistants for 20-40 short sessions over 3-6 months, focusing on vocabulary, narrative and producing more complex sentences.	**Good** evidence this strategy can improve oral language in children who start school with low language skills.	Resources: Language4Reading Academic papers: (Fricke et al. 2013; Bowyer-Crane et al. 2008; Lee and Pring 2016)
Phonological awareness training		A scripted phonological intervention led by teaching assistants for 20-40 short sessions over 3-6 months, focusing on awareness of sounds and letter knowledge.	**Good** evidence that teaching phonological awareness and phonics can help avoid literacy difficulties in children with low language.	Research: (Bower-Crane et al. 2008)
Consultative approach with speech and language therapist		A speech and language therapist gives advice on resources and approaches to use with specific children.	**Moderate** evidence that teachers working with speech and language therapists can improve language outcomes.	Research: (Gallagher and Chiat 2009; Mecrow et al. 2010)
Peer tutoring using story maps		A child with language needs is paired with a more able peer and they work together putting a story into a story map format. Similar to LEGO therapy, described below.	**Promising** evidence that peers working together improves communication skills, although currently based only on children in special schools.	Resources: Story Maps Research: Grunke et al. 2016

Source: Ask Research and Coventry (2017a).

Putting the evidence to work

However, having accessed the research evidence, which is relevant to an issue in your school, there remains the issue that research in itself does not tell you, the practitioner, what to do in your setting. As Dylan Wiliam (2019) argues, the results of a good randomised controlled trial may show what worked 'somewhere', and that in conjunction with certain support factors the intervention may have made a positive contribution for some of the learners involved in the study. On the other hand, there may be a number of learners for whom the intervention may have had a negative impact.

Unfortunately, this information on its own is not much use to you, particularly if your setting is very different from those involved in the study. So if you are going to use a research study to support the use of a research-based intervention in your school, you need to know whether the support factors necessary for the intervention to work – for example, teachers, professional development time, access to resources – are available. If they are, then you may have good reason to think that a particular intervention might work in your setting.

However, even if there does appear to be a 'match' between your setting and the study setting, that only gives you a small part of the information you need before deciding to proceed with the intervention. Cartwright (2019) uses the image of randomised controlled trials and meta-analysis as being 'like the small twigs in a bird's nest. A heap of these twigs will not stay together in the wind. But they can be sculpted together in a tangle of leaves, grass, moss, mud, saliva, and feathers to build a secure nest.'

Implications for teachers of SEND

Given the above, what are the implications for teachers of SEND? Well, if you synthesise the recommendations for teachers for making the most of research from both Cartwright (2019) and Wiliam (2019), it is possible to come up with six questions SEND practitioners and school leaders should ask when trying to use educational research to bring about improvement in schools.

1. Does this 'intervention' solve a problem you need to address?
2. Is your setting similar enough in ways that matter to other settings in which the intervention appears to have worked elsewhere?
3. What other information can you find – be it from other fields and disciplines outside of education or your own knowledge of your school and learners – so you can derive your own model and theory of change of how the intervention could work?

4. What support factors need to be in place for the theory of change and implementation to work in your school?

5. How much improvement will you get? What would success look like? What would failure look like? How often will you review?

6. How much will it cost?

However, for SEND practitioners, even if they are able to come up with plausible answers to these questions, there still remains the problem that individual learners will respond in different ways to different interventions, and research has little to say about why this happens.

Becoming a better evidence-informed SEND practitioner

There's no easy way of becoming an evidence-informed SEND practitioner; it will take time, commitment and hard work, and it is not something that you will ever 'master' or 'crack'. However, if you are committed to learning, displaying a spirit of inquiry, being genuinely curious about what works, and having an open mind, then you will not go far wrong, particularly if you:

- Ask questions about your practice
- Challenge assumptions
- Systematically gather evidence from multiple sources
- Spend time thinking about the trustworthiness of the evidence
- Consider how you can 'weigh up' and pull together the evidence
- Reflect on how you integrate evidence into your decision-making process
- Commit to rigorously evaluating the outcomes of decisions you have made.

References and further reading

Ask Research and Coventry University. (2017a) *SEN Support: research evidence on effective approaches and examples of current practice in good and outstanding schools and colleges*, commissioned by the Department for Education. London: Department for Education.

Ask Research and Coventry University. (2017b) *Effective SEN Support: research evidence on effective approaches and examples of current practice in good and outstanding schools and colleges: A guide for senior leaders in education settings*, commissioned by the Department for Education. London: Department for Education.

Carroll, J. M., Bradley, L., Crawford, H., Hannant, P., Johnson, H. and Thompson, A. (2017) *SEN support: A rapid evidence assessment*. London: Department for Education.

Cartwright, N. and Hardie, J. (2012) *Evidence-based policy: A practical guide to doing it better*. Oxford: Oxford University Press.

Cartwright, N. (2019) 'What is meant by "rigour" in evidence-based educational policy and what's so good about it?' *Educational Research and Evaluation*, 25(1-2): pp. 63–80.

Cullen, M. A., Lindsay, G., Hastings, R., Denne, L., Stanford, C., Beqiraq, L., Elahi, F., Gemegah, E., Hayden, N., Kander, I., Lykomitrou F. and Zander, J. (2020) *Special Educational Needs in mainstream schools: Evidence review*. London: Education Endowment Foundation. Available at: https://educationendowmentfoundation.org.uk/education-evidence/ evidence-reviews/special-educational-needs-and-disabilities-send (Accessed: 27 September 2021).

EEF. (2020) *Special Educational Needs in mainstream schools: Guidance report*. London: Education Endowment Foundation. Available at: https:// d2tic4wvo1iusb.cloudfront.net/guidance-reports/send/EEF_Special_ Educational_Needs_in_Mainstream_Schools_Guidance_Report.pdf (Accessed: 27 September 2021).

Henderson, P. (2018) *EEF Blog: Supporting pupils with SEND – 3 key messages for schools*. Available at: https://educationendowmentfoundation. org.uk/news/eef-blog-supporting-pupils-with-send-what-weve-learned-so-far (Accessed: 4 October 2021).

Johnson, H., Carroll, J. and Bradley, L. (2017) *SEN Support: a survey of schools and colleges*. London: Department for Education.

Jones, G. (2018) *Evidence-based school leadership and management: A practical guide*. London: Sage.

Skipp, A. and Hopwood, V. (2017) *SEN Support: Case studies from schools and college*. London: Department for Education.

Wiliam, D. (2019) 'Why meta-analysis is really hard to do in education.' In The Big Evidence Debate, University of Durham.

PART 2
UNIVERSAL PROVISION

'Every teacher is a teacher of SEND' is a well-known maxim in the English education system. It refers to the SEND Code of Practice (DfE, 2015) and the first steps in the graduated approach where learners with SEND are taught predominantly the same content by the same class teacher as their peers. This section looks at three approaches to this. In chapter 3, Katherine Walsh asks 'What is inclusive teaching and how do you know if you're doing it?' while in chapters 4 and 5, we look at two specific approaches that can be used to support learners with SEND within the mainstream classroom: dual coding and appropriately deployed teaching assistants.

3. WHAT IS INCLUSIVE TEACHING AND HOW DO YOU KNOW IF YOU'RE DOING IT?

KATHERINE WALSH

Katherine Walsh began her teaching career in the United States before continuing in the UK. Katherine is a regional lead for Whole School SEND, runs an Education Endowment Foundation project on inclusion and is inclusion lead for the River Learning Trust.

In her chapter, Katherine explores how teachers in England are routinely asked to teach inclusively, at a 'high quality' and – where necessary – to differentiate for different groups of learners. But does the evidence support these approaches, and in a time-poor environment, what does inclusivity look like in practice?

The importance of 'high-quality' teaching as the first response when supporting children and young people with SEND is underlined in the SEND Code of Practice. Section 6.37 could not be clearer:

> *High quality teaching, differentiated for individual pupils, is the first step in responding to pupils who have or may have SEN. Additional intervention and support cannot compensate for a lack of good quality teaching (DfE, 2015).*

'High quality' and 'differentiated' teaching is positioned as the foundation of all SEND provision. But what exactly does this mean?

Differentiated teaching

This phrase, or simply the single word, 'differentiation' has become synonymous with the teaching of children and young people with SEND. Is differentiation inclusive teaching?

Done poorly, differentiation is seen as teaching to three assumed 'ability levels': Challenge 1, 2, 3; Bronze, Silver, Gold; or even Korma, Tikka, Vindaloo. My second-grade class (early 1990s, New Jersey) used three colours to define the groupings of children by their perceived ability: red, white and blue. 'The colours of the flag' our teacher told us. But as seven-year-olds we understood our groupings had no actual link to the colours of the flag, they were merely labels: our peers working on red were the 'smart' kids, white were in the middle and blue were the bottom of the class. How must it feel to be a child limited to the 'blue' group at seven?

Differentiation is a concept that can result in significant workload for the classroom teacher and does not have clear limits on what adaptations a teacher should reasonably be expected to undertake as part of universal practice. Ashman (2018) has outlined several challenges with the diversity of interpretations of 'differentiation' and the concept has been described as 'under-conceptualised' by Rob Webster and Peter Blatchford (2019).

Is there evidence that differentiation, or differentiated activities, improves outcomes for children and young people despite the potential impacts on the self-esteem of children and the increased workload of the teacher? No – in fact, research evidences that 'providing differentiated teaching, activities or resources, has generally not been shown to have much impact on pupils' attainment' (Ofsted, 2019).

Differentiation can be a detriment to a child's self-esteem, and increases teacher workload without adding impact. Why is the word still so closely linked to the teaching of children and young people with SEND?

Without the word 'differentiation', can 'high quality' teaching stand as the foundation for SEND provision?

High-quality teaching

Section 1.24 of the SEND Code of Practice provides further details about high-quality teaching, which presents two key challenges to the notion of 'high quality' teaching as the foundation for SEND provision:

> *High quality teaching that is differentiated and personalised will meet the individual needs of the majority of children and young people. Some children and young people need educational provision that is additional to or different from this. This is special educational provision under Section 21 of the Children and Families Act 2014. Schools and colleges **must** use their*

*best endeavours to ensure that such provision is made for those who need it.
Special educational provision is underpinned by high quality teaching and
is compromised by anything less* (DfE, 2015).

When referring to 'children and young people with SEND', data evidences that
we are not referring to one or two learners in a class of 30. As we saw in chapter
1, around 2% of learners in state-funded primary and secondary schools have
an EHCP, with a further 12.6% of learners in state-funded primary and 11.5% of
learners in state-funded secondary schools having access to SEN Support (DfE,
2021). Therefore, around four learners in a class of 30 will have an identified
SEND. Consider for a moment a secondary school teacher teaching five lessons
a day – the teacher is likely to be teaching more than 20 learners with SEND
each school day. Without a manageable concept of what high-quality teaching
is, this can be a daunting prospect.

However, thinking about the children and young people with SEND, in a class
of 30, is just a starting point. The Education Policy Institute's analysis of the
2016 GCSE cohort found that, while a maximum of 23% of children and young
people in a year group had SEND at any one time, 39% were recorded with
SEND at some point between Reception and Year 11 (Hutchinson, 2017). For a
class of 30, this signifies that 12 children and young people would be identified
as needing educational provision 'additional to or different from' high-quality
teaching at some point in their school career.

Personalised high-quality teaching

Building on the number of children and young people with potential SEND
within a class, a second challenge to the classroom teacher trying to enact
'high quality' teaching as a first step in responding to learners with SEND
is that each learner is an individual, with individualised life experiences,
strengths, interests, motivations and barriers to learning. An understanding
of the individual is needed for the teacher to be able to deploy effective
teaching strategies and scaffold work appropriately. There is a wealth of
research available to teachers on condition-specific learning needs, but given
that each learner is an individual, what may work for one learner, e.g. a child
with attention deficit hyperactivity disorder (ADHD), may not work for a
different child with ADHD. This challenge persists in both primary and
secondary settings. The challenge in understanding the learning profiles in
secondary school is well established, as teachers may teach 150 children and
young people over the course of a school day. In primary, while some may say
a teacher 'only' needs to teach 30 children over the course of the school day,

the challenge is in effectively scaffolding all areas of the curriculum to a class of diverse learners.

This challenge has been brought to life in Ofsted's Supporting SEND research and analysis, developed to explore how the needs of children and young people are met in mainstream schools. A key finding of the small-scale, qualitative case study (21 learners in seven mainstream schools) is:

> *Schools often took a pupil-centred approach when identifying needs and planning provision, but staff did not always know the pupils well enough to do this* (Ofsted, 2020).

The report explains that 'schools worked towards building secure understandings of pupils and their needs', however 'gaps in understanding of pupils' needs and starting points resulted in a negative impact on their experiences, learning and development' (ibid.).

The challenges with understanding individual learning needs are exemplified in further research conducted by the Education Policy Institute. Their analysis revealed that the primary school a child attends 'makes more difference to their chances of being identified with SEND than anything about them as an individual, their experiences or what local authority they live in' (Hutchinson, 2021).

Despite these challenges, legislation sets out that teachers are 'responsible and accountable for the progress and development of the pupils in their class, including where pupils access support from teaching assistants or specialist staff' (DfE, 2015). Whereas many will think of Teacher Standard 5 as the standard that sets out a teacher's responsibility for the progress and development of children and young people with SEND, this notion is echoed throughout the exemplifications of all of Teachers' Standards, for example:

- 'establish a safe and stimulating environment for pupils, rooted in mutual respect' (Standard 1)
- 'be accountable for pupils' attainment, progress and outcomes' (Standard 2)
- 'demonstrate an understanding of and take responsibility for promoting high standards of literacy … whatever the teacher's specialist subject' (Standard 3)
- 'reflect systematically on the effectiveness of lessons and approaches to teaching' (Standard 4)

- 'manage classes effectively, using approaches which are appropriate to pupils' needs in order to involve and motivate them' (Standard 7).

What is inclusive teaching?

If we look to Teachers' Standard 5, inclusive teaching could be defined as high-quality teaching, which is adapted to respond to the strengths and needs of all children and young people. This is supported by research from Ofsted, which found, unlike differentiation, 'adapting teaching in a responsive way, for example by providing focused support to pupils who are not making progress, is likely to improve outcomes' (Ofsted, 2019).

The Education Endowment Foundation's Special Education Needs in Mainstream Schools Guidance report sets out in its foreword:

It is tempting to talk about the challenge of SEND as a specific and distinct issue. Yet, far from creating new programmes, the evidence tells us that teachers should instead prioritise familiar but powerful strategies, like scaffolding and explicit instruction, to support their pupils with SEND (EEF, 2020).

The notion of inclusive teaching as high-quality teaching, adapted to respond to the strengths and needs of all learners, is further emphasised in Recommendations 3 and 4:

- 'Ensure all pupils have access to high quality teaching.'
- 'Complement high quality teaching with carefully selected small-group and one-to-one interventions.'

Recommendation 4 is of particular importance when thinking about inclusive teaching. In many instances children and young people with SEND will spend large parts of the school day working with a teaching assistant, or in pull-out interventions. For inclusive teaching to occur, these interventions need to complement high-quality teaching – teaching assistants should not be used as 'an informal instructional resource for pupils in most need':

It is important [that teaching assistants] add value to the work of the teacher, not replace them – the expectation should be that the needs of all pupils are addressed, first and foremost, through high quality classroom teaching (EEF, 2018).

Ofsted's research for the Education Inspection Framework draws on decades of research to comprehensively outline both the importance of, and what is, 'effective teaching'. Teachers should adapt their teaching through, for example, scaffolding learning tasks or focused support to individuals or groups of learners within a lesson, before considering pull-out interventions. Research evidences that learners' attainment is 'strongly affected by the quantity and pacing of instruction' (Ofsted, 2019). Careful planning of lessons is therefore needed to ensure all children and young people have the 'opportunity to learn'. What does this look like in practice?

Inclusive teaching in practice

This brings us back to a challenge presented earlier, that an average class will have four children and young people with identified SEND, and potentially 12 requiring educational provision 'additional to or different from' high-quality teaching at some point in their school career. How can a teacher plan a lesson for a class of 30, that ensures all children and young people have the opportunity to learn?

All children and young people will progress at different rates; this includes children and young people with and without SEND. Thinking through your class by labels (e.g. two children with autism, one child with dyslexia, one child with SEMH, six Pupil Premium children), can be overwhelming and unhelpful. Instead, focus your attention on learning about the individuals in your class, seeing diagnostic labels as a starting point for further enquiry. This process starts as soon as you find out the class(es) you are teaching next year – talk to the teacher(s) who had the class, or individual learners, previously. How did they adapt their teaching to respond to the strengths and needs of all learners? Take note of the strategies they employed.

Children and young people with SEND will often have additional information about their learning needs that can support your adaptive teaching. Some children and young people will have an EHCP that lists the provision that needs to be provided to meet their special educational needs. For children and young people with SEN Support, each school will have its own method of recording information about the learner, including information about their barriers to learning and recommended teaching strategies and resources. If you do not have access to this information, talk to the SENCO. The SENCO will be able to direct you to further information about the learner. This may include an individual provision plan or a report from an external agency, e.g. educational psychology or speech and language therapy.

As you find out more about the children and young people in your class, you will find common teaching strategies that you can employ to support their collective access. These strategies can then be employed to adapt your teaching so that it responds to the strengths and needs of all. This will take time – secondary school teachers will need to undertake this process for each class that they teach. Doing this as a proactive process, so that you are as prepared as you can be in your first lesson can, and often will, save you time over the course of the school year. If, as a part of this process, there is a learner you are particularly worried about, start building a relationship with the child or young person as soon as you can. This can support the transition process, and when the child or young person enters your classroom for their first lesson, there will be a level of familiarity which can support the learner's access to your teaching.

Clarity of presentation is a crucial component to high-quality teaching: effective teachers are 'able to communicate clearly and directly with their pupils' (Ofsted, 2019). How can you adapt your teaching to ensure all children and young people are able to access your teaching? Consider adapting your lessons by using visual supports – visuals can benefit children and young people with many different types of SEND, including but not limited to autism, ADHD, developmental language disorder and hearing impairment. Based on the learning needs of the children and young people in your class, could it be beneficial to have a visual timetable of your lesson, with additional visual prompts at transition points within the lesson? Would certain learners benefit from visuals, such as a worked example on a maths worksheet, to help them remember the steps needed to solve a problem, when working independently?

Effective questioning and feedback are two further key components to consider when planning and delivering high-quality teaching (Ofsted, 2019). How can you adapt your lessons to ensure all children and young people are able to access class discussions? Reflect on the learning needs of the children and young people in your class – are there some children who need additional time to take notes from the board into their books? This can be a challenging task for many children and young people with SEND, including children with dyslexia, physical disabilities, anxiety and visual impairments. Could printing out key slides for children and young people to take notes on support a number of children and young people to better access your teaching?

Inclusive teaching – how do I know if I am doing it?

Inclusive teaching – as the foundation of SEND provision – requires teachers to notice the children and young people in their class, and reflect on what they see.

As we get to know the children and young people better, we are able to refine our teaching further to better meet the needs of all. When further adaptations are needed to support an individual learner, teachers should use the graduated approach as a framework to develop a better understanding of the child or young person's needs. As outlined in the SEND Code of Practice (DfE, 2015), the graduated approach is a four-part cycle – assess, plan, do, review – with the child or young person at the centre. As a part of the process, 'earlier decisions and actions are revisited, refined and revised with a growing understanding of the pupil's needs and of what supports the pupil in making good progress and securing good outcomes' (DfE, 2015). The voice of the child or young person and their family is an important part of the process, and we should seek their views and feedback our observations to them.

For teaching that includes all children and young people to be realised, collaboration is essential. Classroom teachers should seek advice from colleagues, such as subject leaders and heads of department, to understand the curriculum design and support their decision making in delivering and adapting the curriculum to effectively meet the needs of all learners. A teacher can seek advice from the SENCO, or a colleague who has previously taught a learner in their class, to help them through sharing teaching strategies that enabled them to personalise and scaffold the learning and enabled the learner to access and make progress in the curriculum.

There is no 'one-size-fits-all' checklist to work through to know with certainty that your teaching is fully inclusive. Each child we teach is an individual, and no two children, or classes, are the same. An inclusive teacher is a reflective teacher; the importance of taking the time to notice the children and young people in our classrooms and understand where exactly they are in the curriculum cannot be overstated. A useful framework to reflect on your practice is the SEND Reflection Framework (Whole School SEND).

As a starting point, five areas I take time to reflect on when both teaching, and supporting other teachers, are:

1. Knowledge of the learner: What do you know about the children and young people you are teaching? Think through the children and young people you teach – for learners that stand out as those you may not 'know' yet:

   - Do you know (and understand) their individual strengths, interests, motivations and barriers to learning?

- Have you talked with the child or young person about their learning?
- Are you in conversation with their parents/carers? Can the child's family help you better understand the learner?
- Have you spoken to your colleagues – teachers who have previously taught the child, or a teacher who is currently teaching the child in a different subject? What has your colleague learned about the child or young person, how do they scaffold the curriculum, and what teaching strategies do they find beneficial to the child or young person?

2. Creating an inclusive environment: Is your classroom an environment conducive to learning? Take time to observe the children and young people in the classroom – how do they interact with the environment, with each other? Are all children socially included? Sit in a child's seat: how accessible is the classroom from their perspective?

3. Curriculum expertise: In order to effectively scaffold the curriculum, we need to be experts in the subject we are teaching. Are there parts of the curriculum you are less confident in teaching? If the answer is yes, what steps can you take to better understand the content so that you can then effectively scaffold it for your learners?

4. Strategies to scaffold learning: Have you embedded the graduated approach (assess, plan, do, review) as a part of your teaching practice? There is a wealth of condition-specific advice and recommendations available for free online (the SEND Gateway is a useful starting point: https://www.sendgateway.org.uk/resources). Have you trialled recommended teaching strategies within your lessons? What was the impact?

5. Your wellbeing: In addition to reflecting on your learners, are you taking the time to reflect on how you are feeling? As discussed throughout this chapter, there are many challenges to the role, and at times the task at hand can feel overwhelming. If you are feeling this way, what are the systems in place within your school to support you, and your wellbeing? If you are not sure, ask. Your wellbeing is of utmost importance.

Inclusive teaching is a challenge – but we need to see it as an opportunity. Not only is it an opportunity to grow, to continually improve our teaching – if we get inclusive teaching right, we are making a significant difference to the children and young people we teach. We are supporting those that need the most precise and expert teaching to progress; something that, I believe, is the reason most of us decided to teach in the first place. Let's not let the challenges of inclusive teaching make us lose sight of the opportunities – as teachers, we have the opportunity, the potential, to positively impact the life trajectories of the children and young people we teach.

References and further reading

Ashman, G. (2018) *Is it time to ditch 'differentiation'?* Available at: www. cem.org/blog/is-it-time-to-ditch-differentiation/ (Accessed: 30 June 2021).

Department for Education. (DfE) CooperGibson Research, corp creators. (2018) *Factors affecting teacher retention: qualitative investigation.* [Research Report] London: DfE.

Department for Education. (2013) *Teachers' Standards.* London: DfE.

Department for Education. (2015) *Special educational needs and disability code of practice: 0 to 25 years.* London: DfE.

Department for Education. (2021) *Special educational needs in England: January 2021.* Available at: www.gov.uk/government/statistics/special-educational-needs-in-england-january-2021 (Accessed: 30 June 2021).

Education Endowment Foundation. (2018) *Making best use of teaching assistants: Guidance report.* Available at: https:// educationendowmentfoundation.org.uk/public/files/Publications/ Teaching_Assistants/TA_Guidance_Report_MakingBestUseOfTeachingA ssistants-Printable.pdf (Accessed: 30 June 2021).

Education Endowment Foundation. (2020) *Special Educational Needs in mainstream schools: Guidance report.* Available at: https:// educationendowmentfoundation.org.uk/public/files/Publications/Send/ EEF_Special_Educational_Needs_in_Mainstream_Schools_Guidance_ Report.pdf (Accessed: 30 June 2021).

Hutchinson, J. (2017) *How many children have SEND?* Available at: https:// epi.org.uk/publications-and-research/many-children-send/ (Accessed: 30 June 2021).

Hutchinson, J. (2021) *Identifying pupils with special educational needs and disabilities.* Available at: https://epi.org.uk/publications-and-research/ identifying-send/ (Accessed: 30 June 2021).

Ofsted. (2019) *Education inspection framework: Overview of research.* Available at: www.gov.uk/government/publications/education-inspection-framework-overview-of-research (Accessed: 30 June 2021).

Ofsted. (2021) *Supporting SEND.* Available at: www.gov.uk/government/publications/supporting-send/supporting-send (Accessed: 30 June 2021).

Webster, R. and Blatchford, P. (2019) 'Making sense of "teaching", "support" and "differentiation": the educational experiences of pupils with Education, Health and Care Plans and Statements in mainstream secondary schools.' *European Journal of Special Needs Education*, 34(1): pp. 98–113.

Whole School SEND Reflection Framework. Available at: www.sendgateway.org.uk/resources/send-reflection-framework (Accessed: 30 June 2021).

Whole School SEND. SEND gateway: Resources and Publications. Available at: www.sendgateway.org.uk/resources. (Accessed: 30 June 2021).

4. DUAL CODING: THE BIG WINS FOR LEARNERS WITH SEND

OLIVER CAVIGLIOLI

Oliver Caviglioli has spent a large part of his career as headteacher of a special school. While he now specialises in visualising educational concepts and processes, for this chapter he has drawn on some of his knowledge – and even a publication – from the earlier part of his career.

Oliver leads us through the theory and concepts of dual coding considering how and when this pedagogical approach may best be applied in mainstream classrooms, particularly to the benefit of learners with SEND.

Decades of research led cognitive scientist, Richard E Mayer, to conclude that 'people learn better from graphics and words than from words alone'. Is this any more significant for learners with SEND? And, if so, what should be happening in the classroom?

Integrating dual coding into teaching practices directly helps learners assimilate new information into their schema and assists in its later retrieval

Dual coding theory is experiencing something of a revival at the moment, in the wake of the UK schools' tardy appreciation of cognitive science. Devised by Allan Paivio nearly half a century ago (Paivio, 1971), the theory has been subject to continuous research over the decades and emerges as a convincingly robust description of how humans process both verbal and visual information.

For some evolutionary purpose, humans have separate channels in which to receive and process visual and verbal stimuli. Separate and independent as they may be, they nonetheless also manage to relate to one another in a way that Paivio described as 'associative links' (Paivio, 1990). It is the nature of these connections that provides the doubling of encoding power, described by Paul Kirschner as 'double-barrelled learning' (Kirschner, 2019). This is because by forming such cross-channel connections, this naturally occurring phenomenon is said to double the memory traces within long-term memory. As a consequence, there is a doubling of the chances of it being retrieved, as the memory hook can be either the visual or the verbal component. In this sense, as John Sweller remarks, 'Working memory capacity can be effectively increased, and learning improved, by using a dual mode presentation' (Sweller et al., 2011). Dual mode is the equivalent term for dual coding within cognitive load theory's lexicon.

The diagram below – following the protocols of dual-coded explanations – represents the major dynamics of dual coding theory. There are, however, certain modifications. While Paivio describes the objects of verbal and visual processing as imagens and logogens, I find these terms unnecessary for teachers to adopt. More useful is to substitute the metaphors proposed by Baddeley and Hitch's (1974) memory model – the visuospatial sketch pad and the auditory loop. Such metaphors represent the limited capacity of these information channels within working memory. The additional visual metaphor of the radio waves signifies the 'associative links' that exist between them. Below the visuospatial sketchpad and the auditory loop are two icons that symbolise the different structures of these two channels. The nature of the differences and their significance to teachers of learners with SEND is key to exploiting to the full the power of dual coding.

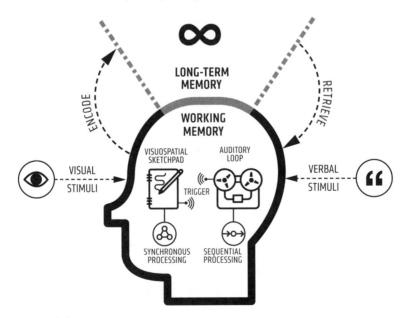

Source: Caviglioli, 2019.

There is more to dual coding than simply combining words and images for richer encoding and more proficient retrieval

That is not to dismiss nor devalue this very powerful way of mitigating, to some extent, the limitations of our working memory. With our working memory capacity judged to be around four elements (Cowan, 2001), enabling such a doubling of encoding and retrieval potential is a terrific boon to learning, particularly for learners with SEND. It is not a question of achieving some sort of abstract level of optimum efficiency applicable to all learners but, rather, recognising that children with SEND have the capacity to double their own potential in this area. However, when discussing this phenomenon, writers rarely mention that throughout Paivio's research in this area, the nature of the material his subjects were asked to process was cognitively unchallenging. It seems to have paralleled his predecessor, Herman Ebbinghaus (1885), in not involving any computational aspect. For both, it was a question of retrieval alone, pure and simple.

But, of course, classrooms are not like that. While the retrieval of isolated facts is belatedly acknowledged as having a valid – indeed important – part in classroom practice, its role is subsidiary to the development of understanding, expressed in terms of schema formation. In this respect, we can think of a memory continuum with Ebbinghaus' focus on simple material at one end and Frederick Bartlett's seminal work (Bartlett, 1932) on schemas at the other. A parallel contrast can be drawn with Paivio's work. At one end is the focus on the pairing of verbal and visual stimuli for effective retrieval, and at the other end is the part that mirrors Bartlett's concentration on meaning-making.

While Paivio was examining the nature of the two separate information channels, he noted that they differed in structure. Verbal information – logogens in Paivio's terminology – was sequential in nature and, as such, 'subject to the same sequential processing constraints' (Paivio, 1990). By this, Paivio explains that we can identify short groups of up to three or four letters, rather akin to our in-born ability to subitise a very small number of objects (Kaufman et al., 1949). Any more and we start to be cognitively challenged, due to the demands of the syntax that binds the separate words together. By contrast, Paivio described visual information as being organised in a synchronous, or simultaneous manner (Paivio, 1990). This means that the observer can note several components of the visual at the same time. And their perception is accompanied by a natural ability to read their spatial configurations meaningfully and automatically. This contrast between the two sensory systems – as exploited in their pairing for simple retrieval purposes – and their differing structures which are significant in terms of understanding, can be mirrored with the memory continuum described above.

Providing learners with diagrams to accompany teacher explanations or texts is a type of cognitive scaffolding that particularly benefits learners with SEND, or with low prior knowledge.

We are at the point when we can appreciate that dual coding's power of tethering visual and verbal information is only really half the story. Psychologists followed up on Paivio's distinguishing the structural differences between verbal and visual information. Larkin and Simon (1987) wrote a paper titled *Why a Diagram is (Sometimes) Worth Ten Thousand Words*, in which they developed Waller's (1981) notion of The Visual Argument. They contrasted 'diagrammatic from sentential paper-and-pencil representations of information … that are informationally equivalent' by testing people's speed and accuracy of understanding. Their conclusion was that diagrams are often 'computationally more efficient'. Vekiri (2002) explains it this way:

> … *graphical displays organize information spatially. When all the important information is grouped together in a display, it can be easily located. Users do not have to store any data in working memory because the necessary data are always available in the display and are easily retrieved.*

In their comprehensive survey of the use of graphics in the learning process, Clark and Lyons (2004) state that for learners with low prior knowledge (the sometimes alternative description of SEND), visuals can aid understanding, explaining: 'for higher-level learning, most benefit from the use of explanatory visual representations of content that are congruent with text because the visual can reduce load and provide a secondary route to forming mental models,' referencing the following studies: Cuevas, Fiore and Oser (2002); Gyselinck and Tardieu (1999); Mayer and Gallini (1990).

Research – as the teaching profession has reluctantly come to accept – doesn't always offer us clear messages

In contrast to the above reports of the benefits of visual communication to learners with SEND, Vekiri (2002), in her review of the educational value of graphic displays, notes that Hegarty et al. (1991), and Hegarty and Just (1993) 'provide a different perspective'. These researchers, by collecting data on learners' eye-fixations, found that learners with higher prior knowledge were better able to exploit the potential of diagrams by frequently switching from visual to text in order to extend and monitor their growing comprehension. 'High-knowledge participants were more capable of locating the relevant information in a diagram and extract information more selectively' (Hegarty and Just, 1989).

Mayer and Gallini (1990) found the opposite: that the high-knowledge learners did not gain as much from the inclusion of diagrams as did those with SEND. More recently, the same Mayer, along with his colleague Fiorella (Fiorella and Mayer, 2015) in their book, *Learning As A Generative Activity*, analysed the results of around 25 to 35 studies for the boundary conditions of the use of mapping (a collective term for concept maps, knowledge maps and graphic organisers). They found that 'the mapping effect is strongest when learners are low in experience or ability (d=0.45 based on four comparisons) rather than high (d=-0.08 based on four comparisons).' In addition, they advise that 'younger learners may benefit from guidance during learning such as providing partially completed maps.'

To add another dimension, researchers have found that learners vary in their visuospatial abilities. This is unrelated to general cognitive ability and has nothing to do with the myth of learning styles. Nonetheless, it presents as a barrier to learners faced with a visual model. Clark and Lyons (2004) recommend teachers 'provide visual support for low spatial aptitude learners when tasks require spatial ability'. Along with their stark reminder that 'visuals ignored don't teach', this should prompt teachers to take time to explain how exactly one reads a diagram, ensuring the part of the diagram being analysed is clearly signalled to the learners.

The spatial component of the visuospatial domain has been largely ignored when discussing SEND, but it yields important insights into how to increase learners' access to knowledge.

Over a dozen years ago, I wrote an article with Tina Detheridge – creator of an app for digital symbols for writing – on the use of symbols in special schools (Caviglioli and Detheridge, 2006). In it, we wrote that the use of a symbol word processor, however plausibly attractive, does not address the issue of the complexity of the syntax of sentences – the sentential organisation defined by Larkin and Simon (1987). If subjects with no SEND were found to overload their cognitive resources by going back and forth along sentences in order to make sense, how much more would this be the case for learners with SEND?

By contrast, there was common agreement that where symbols were most effective in conveying information in the most efficient way was in their use in visual timetables. Here is one such example:

Source: Caviglioli, 2019.

As I explain in Dual Coding With Teachers (2019):

> *With the matrix timetable we process so much more information in so much easier a fashion. Locating the swimming activity tells you the day and time. It also tells you what comes before and after it, as well as what was on the day before and after at the same time. That means that, at a glance, with very little effort, four pieces of information are immediately known. Think how complex a verbal description would have been.*

Or as Barwise and Etchemendy (1990) explain, '... the diagram can generate a lot of information that the user never need infer. Rather, the user can simply read off facts from the diagram as needed. This situation is in stark contrast to sentential inference, where even the most trivial consequence needs to be inferred explicitly.'

Reorganising knowledge into diagrammatic, two-dimensional arrangements has further cognitive benefits – cognitive offloading and embodied cognition

In text, each element (i.e. word) is adjacent to only the previous and next in the linear sequence, whereas in a diagram, elements can share the same location and be adjacent to very many other elements. Their relationships are concrete and self-evident, and don't require the heavy cognitive inference that is demanded of text. So while diagrams and text are both visible, it is only the former that frees up cognitive resources to allow for deeper explorations. The external representation of a diagram parallels the non-linear schema that contain the meaning. As such, the transmission of meaning to the viewer of the diagram is more direct.

For learners with SEND, perhaps with a more restricted working memory capacity, this means that less time and effort is spent in searching for related items in sentences and making the required inferences. Access to the key meaning, it could be said, has been democratised. Alongside this huge benefit, diagrams are able to integrate aspects of embodied cognition (Barsalou, 2008). Once considered outside the sphere of cognitive psychology, the use of gestures in the form of drawing and tracing have recently been acknowledged to play a significant supportive role in learning. So much so, in fact, that Sweller and colleagues (2011) have included both as part of his cognitive load theory. Human movement, it transpires, is also a form of cognitive offloading, adding to the richness of the encoding process while causing minimal cognitive load (Risko and Gilbert, 2016).

More specifically, we learn that drawing is the most effective of all mnemonic devices to remember learned vocabulary, according to Fernandes and colleagues (2018), and that tracing, with the index finger, the angles of a geometric problem produces higher learning outcomes than not doing so (Hu et al., 2015).

Listing the benefits of dual coding reads like a bill of rights for all learners – and a guaranteed entitlement for those with SEND

In her comprehensive summary of research into visual displays, Vekiri (2002) notes that learners with low prior knowledge benefit more from the use of visuals than their classmates with more expertise. This analysis is borne out by Fiorella and Mayer (2015) in the ground-breaking book *Learning As A Generative Activity* in which they focus on eight cognitive strategies. Among these techniques, we find the dual coding approaches of mapping, drawing, enacting (i.e. manipulating) and imagining, all of which prove also to be supportive when combined with some of the other strategies — summarising, self-explanation and teaching.

As unusual as this list is, the most pertinent aspect of their work is the inclusion of boundary conditions of each one of the approaches. With regards to mapping, for instance, we learn that 'mapping appears to be more effective for lower-ability students than for higher-ability students', and that 'mapping appears to be more effective for young readers when more support is provided during learning than when little support is provided.'

These findings appear to be borne out by Vekiri: we learn that 'the learning effects of diagrams may be a function of the interaction of their characteristics and learners' prior knowledge' and that 'students with low prior knowledge about mechanical devices benefited more from the diagrams than high-knowledge students.' However, there seems to be an element of Goldilocks in the degree of low prior knowledge involved, as cognitive science authors Clark and Lyons in their classic *Graphics for Learning* (2004) identify that learners' too low prior knowledge negates the benefits of diagrams. This view is echoed by Cheng and colleagues (2001) when they write: '… without a certain minimum knowledge of the domain, an individual is unlikely to be able to use a domain-specific diagram effectively.'

While the use of dual coding for learners with SEND can be hugely supportive, there are constraints and protocols that need integrating into teachers' knowledge base

Clark and Lyons (2004) identify the two features of learners that limit the impact of dual coding: too low, or no, relevant prior knowledge, and too low a level of visuospatial skills. The latter, not to be misidentified as part of the learning skills mythology, does exist. Clark and Lyons, however, point out that teachers can teach their learners how to read a diagram, noting that they should clearly signal which part of the diagram they are commenting on, in order to avoid the learner forever searching for the focus of the teachers' commentary.

Alongside this, Clark and Lyons point out two aspects of teaching that inhibit learners from fully benefiting from dual coding practice. One is the wrong choice of visuals. For example, when dealing with a process, at whatever scale, a mind map, or tree diagram would be an inappropriate choice. A flow chart or timeline would be the far better choice. The following table identifies attempts over several decades from different authors to create a rationale for the choice of graphic organiser.

	STASIS [CLUSTER]		CHANGE [ORDER]	
PEHRSSON & DENNER Semantic Organizers 1989				
COOPER Think and Link 1979	CLASSIFICATION	COMPARISON & CONTRAST	SEQUENCING	CAUSE & EFFECT
WALKER Sentences and the Web of Knowledge 2018	CATEGORIES	COMPARISON	SEQUENCE IN TIME	CAUSE & EFFECT
MARZANO et al Classroom Instruction that Works 2001	CONCEPT GENERALIZATION PRINCIPLE		TIME SEQUENCE	PROCESS CAUSE/EFFECT EPISODE
HYLERLE Visual Tools for Constructing Knowledge 1996	CLASSIFYING PART-WHOLE	COMPARING & CONTRASTING	SEQUENCING	CAUSE & EFFECT
WRAGG & BROWN Explaining 1993	CONCEPTS		PROCEDURES PROCESSES	CAUSE & EFFECT CONSEQUENCES
MOHAN Language and Content 1986	CLASSIFICATION	EVALUATION DESCRIPTION	SEQUENCE	PRINCIPLES
CAVIGLIOLI Dual Coding With Teachers 2019	**CHUNK**	**COMPARE**	**SEQUENCE**	**CAUSE & EFFECT**

Graphic organiser choices. Source: Caviglioli, 2019.

Assuming the teacher has selected the appropriate graphic organiser for the task at hand, there remains the second reason why their efforts might become less than effective: poor execution. At this point, the pedagogical domain overlaps with that of graphic principles. From the many visual displays, diagrams, posters and slides I am requested to comment on with regard to improvement, I have identified four main faults that help shape my responses. I offer my guidance in this way:

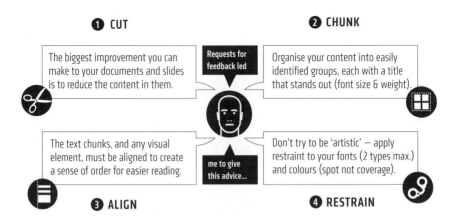

Guidance for creating graphics in education. Source: Caviglioli, 2019.

Working from Paivio's research, Richard E Mayer has tested its application and, in doing so, has arrived at a set of principles that help teachers fully exploit the impact of dual coding in their classrooms

Not adhering to the principles listed below might cause only mere annoyance or a slight hiccup in the learning of high-achieving learners. For learners with SEND, by contrast, they might become stumbling blocks. The major principles directly related to teaching learners with SEND are:

The Coherence Principle: students learn more effectively when the visual used doesn't contain any distracting, irrelevant elements. This is the most straightforward of the principles, the easiest to implement and the one with the biggest impact.

The Signalling Principle: this entails the explicit pointing to specific parts of a visual being explained either in writing or speech. Failure to do this results in students wasting their valuable and limited cognitive resources in searching.

The Redundancy Principle: students will learn more effectively if visuals are teamed with speech rather than text. The basis for this being that text and visuals occupy the same channel whereas the visual and speech combination is spread over two channels.

The Spatial Continuity Principle: similar to cognitive load's split-attention effect, this requires that text is not separated from the visual it is referring to.

The Temporal Contiguity Principles: narratives related to visuals should be coordinated in order to avoid a student having to keep in mind either the visual while listening to the narrative, or vice versa.

The Segmenting Principle: students learn more effectively when they are not overwhelmed by the information presented. Instead it is more effective to break it down into smaller chunks.

The Pre-Training Principle: another way to avoid students being overwhelmed by too much unfamiliar information is to introduce it gradually, ensuring, for example, that key vocabulary and concepts are clarified from the start.

Adopting and integrating visual strategies to support students with SEND makes teaching clearer and more effective for all

In his foreword to Clark and Lyons' *Graphics for Learning* (2004), Richard Mayer's first sentence stated that 'people learn better from graphics and words than from words alone.' From someone who has conducted research studies in this area for several decades, Mayer's conclusion comes with an authority that can reassure mainstream teachers that an emphasis on visual strategies benefits all learners in the class. Energy now needs to move on to the question of how best to execute and apply them.

References and further reading

Baddeley, A. D. and Hitch, G. J. (1974) 'Working memory.' In: Bower, G. H. (ed.) *The psychology of learning and motivation: Advances in research and theory.* New York: Academic Press, 51, 5 pp. 267–272.

Barsalou, L. (2008) 'Grounded cognition.' *The Annual Review of Psychology*, 59: pp. 617–645.

Bartlett, F. (1932) *Remembering: A study in experimental and social psychology.* Cambridge: Cambridge University Press.

Barwise, J. and Etchemendy, J. (1991) 'Visual information and valid reasoning.' In: Zimmerman, W. and Cunningham, S. (eds.) *Visualization in teaching and learning mathematics.* Washington, DC: Mathematical Association of America, MMA Notes Series 10–24.

Caviglioli, O. (2019) *Dual coding with teachers.* Woodbridge: John Catt.

Caviglioli, O. and Detheridge, T. (2006) 'Making ideas come alive.' *Special Children*, February/March, pp. 18–20.

Cheng, P. C. H., Lowe, R. K. and Scaife, M. (2001) 'Cognitive science approaches to understanding diagrammatic representations.' In: Blackwell, A. F. (ed.) *Thinking with diagrams.* London: Kluwer Academic Publishers, pp. 79–94.

Clark, R. C. and Lyons, C. (2004) *Graphics for learning.* San Francisco: Pfeiffer.

Cowan, N. (2001) 'The magical number 4 in short-term memory: A reconsideration of mental storage capacity.' *Behavioural and Brain Sciences*, 24: pp. 87–114.

Cuevas, H. M., Fiore, S. M. and Oser, R. L. (2002) 'Scaffolding cognitive and metacognitive processes in low verbal ability learners: Use of diagrams in computer-based training environments.' *Instructional Science*, 30: pp. 433–464.

Ebbinghaus, H. (1885) *Memory: a contribution to experimental psychology.* Dover, New York.

Fernandes, M. A., Wammes, J. D. and Meade, M. E. (2018) 'The surprisingly powerful influence of drawing on memory.' *Current Directions in Psychological Science*, (27)5: pp. 302–308.

Fiorella, L. and Mayer, R. E. (2015) *Learning as a generative activity.* Cambridge University Press.

Gyselinck, V. and Tardieu, H. (1999) 'The role of illustrations in text comprehension: What, when, for whom, and why?' In: van Oostendorp, H. and Goldman, S. R. (eds.) (1998) *The construction of mental representations during reading.* Hillside, NJ: Lawrence Erlbaum.

Hu, F., Ginns, P. and Bobis, J. (2015) 'Getting the point: Tracing worked examples enhances learning.' *Learning and Instruction*, 35: pp. 85–93.

Kaufmann, E. L., Lord, M. W., Reese, T. W. and Volkmann, J. (1949) 'The discrimination of visual number.' *The American Journal of Psychology*, 62(4): pp. 498–525.

Kirschner, P. (2019) 'Dual coding: Double-barrelled learning.' In: Caviglioli, O. *Dual coding with teachers.* Woodbridge: John Catt, pp. 20–21.

Larkin, J. H. and Simon, H. A. (1987) 'Why a diagram is (sometimes) worth ten thousand words.' *Cognitive Science*, 11(1): pp. 65–100.

Mayer, R. E. and Gallini, J. K. (1990) 'When is an illustration worth ten thousand words?' *Journal of Educational Psychology*, 82(4): pp. 715–726.

Mayer, R. E., Heiser, J. and Lonn, S. (2001) 'Cognitive constraints on multimedia learning: When presenting more material results in less understanding.' *Journal of Educational Psychology*, 93(1): pp. 187–198.

Paivio, A. (1971) *Imagery and verbal processes*. New York: Holt, Reinhart and Winston.

Paivio, A. (1990) *Mental representations: A dual coding approach*. New York: Oxford Science Publications, p. 61.

Risko, E. F. and Gilbert, S. J. (2016) 'Cognitive offloading.' *Trends in Cognitive Sciences*, 20(9): pp. 676–688.

Sweller, J., Ayres, P. and Kalyuga, S. (2011) *Cognitive load theory*. New York: Springer.

Vekiri, I. (2002) 'What is the value of graphical displays in learning?' *Educational Psychology Review*, 14(3).

Waller, R. (1981) *Understanding Network Diagrams*. Paper presented at the Annual Meeting of the American Educational Research Association. Los Angeles, April 1981.

5. MAXIMISING THE ROLE, CONTRIBUTION AND IMPACT OF TEACHING ASSISTANTS

MATTHEW PARKER AND ROB WEBSTER

Rob Webster is an Associate Professor, based in the Centre for Inclusive Education, UCL Institute of Education and Matthew Parker is a school improvement consultant and expert adviser for inclusion. Between them, they have extensively researched the employment, deployment and impact of teaching assistants in schools in England and bring this experience to bear in this chapter.

The authors explore the surprising 2009 finding that support from teaching assistants can have a negative impact on academic progress. Contextualising this for supporting learners with SEND in a mainstream classroom, the authors propose five layers of support, to encourage the greatest level of independence possible, with the teaching assistants providing the least help first.

Teaching assistants are an intrinsic part of universal provision in almost every mainstream school, and an essential component of effective inclusion for children and young people with special educational needs, but to what extent are they (and should they be) deployed to effectively support these learners?

Teaching assistants: the currency of SEND provision

The relatively rapid increase in teaching assistant (TA) numbers over the last 20 years represents a significant, though rarely commented on, cultural and structural change to the English school system. At the most recent count (November 2019), 28% of the school workforce in England were TAs. On the basis of this headcount, there are almost as many TAs in our mainstream schools (~332,500) as the entire population of Sunderland.

Such is the vital role of TAs in the day-to-day functioning of SEND provision in mainstream settings, that it is difficult to imagine school life without them: they provide support to individuals with needs of varying complexity and to small groups of learners at risk of falling behind in their learning. For mainstream settings, provision for children and young people with Education, Health and Care Plans (about one in five learners with SEND have needs complex enough to require an EHCP) is commonly quantified in terms of hours of TA support, and this has become the major currency of inclusion. But how good is the exchange rate?

What research tells us: breaking down unconscious segregation

The large-scale Deployment and Impact of Support Staff (DISS) project, conducted over six years, remains the most comprehensive UK study into the deployment and effectiveness of TAs (Blatchford, Russell and Webster, 2012). The impact analysis at the heart of the study involving 8,200 learners in primary and secondary schools was designed to provide reliable data on the effect of TA support on learning outcomes, and controlled for potentially confounding factors, such as prior attainment and SEND status. The findings, published in 2009, challenged conventional and widespread practice by providing evidence of a negative impact of TA support on academic progress. Specifically, it found that the greater the amount of TA support a child received, the less progress they made in English and maths.

The key explanatory factors for the relationship between TA support and learner outcomes were found to relate not to TAs, but to the decisions made about their deployment and the quality of their preparation. Crucially, these are factors outside the control of TAs. Any attribution of 'fault with' or 'blame on' TAs is therefore misplaced. Evidence from the DISS project revealed that while TAs had taken on a greater instructional role than had historically been the case, their conditions of employment, training and preparation had not kept pace with this evolution.

TAs' hours of work, for example, were found to limit opportunities to meet, plan, and prepare with teachers. Teachers similarly felt unprepared by their own training to manage and direct TAs, a finding consistently reflected in the Department for Education's national survey of the preparedness of newly qualified teachers. The DISS project also found that the 'default setting' for TA deployment – supporting lower-attainers and those with SEND – leads to a separation effect: compared to their typically-developing peers, those in most need get less time with the teacher and more time with the least qualified members of staff, plus they receive a lower-quality pedagogical diet. These findings have been replicated in subsequent research.

To reiterate, TAs have very little control over the construction of their role and the circumstances of their employment and deployment. Unpicking these factors is a leadership responsibility, and prompted by the DISS project findings, some schools have addressed this in reshaping their principles, policies and practices. So, while at first pass the DISS results make for dispiriting reading, they have focused minds and helped schools to sharpen practice, shining a light on where and how improvements can be made.

Changing paradigms, rethinking roles

Our Maximising the Impact of Teaching Assistants (MITA) initiative, that builds directly and purposefully on the DISS project findings, encourages teachers and TAs to consider their distinct but complimentary roles and responsibilities in meeting the needs of learners. We encourage school leaders to orchestrate a whole-school discussion in order to arrive at a collective view of what the scope, potential and limits of the TA role ought to be, and to critically explore how teachers and TAs can work together in classroom partnerships.

Teachers hold primary responsibility for learners with SEND; the first line of defence in meeting learners' needs is through high-quality, teacher-led teaching. We start, therefore, from the premise that struggling learners should receive at least as much time with the teacher. To make this possible, the TA's key purpose is to add value to the teacher and their teaching. Well thought through structures and classroom routines between teachers and TAs make for effective, responsive partnerships. TAs can triage problems allowing the teacher space to work with small groups of learners. Effective classroom partnerships work as a tag-team in response to in-class assessment, rotate between groups and share information and feedback during the lesson and through quick, practical reporting systems.

Changing pedagogy: defining support

By defining teacher and TA roles and responsibilities, schools engage with a central issue of ensuring successful universal provision: understanding what effective TA support should and should not look like, and how that is exemplified in the moment-by-moment interactions they have with learners. Research on classroom interactions between TAs and learners shows that TAs tend to focus on task correction and completion. Without clear direction, training and on-going support, these habits can become ingrained and foster learner dependence. Often quite vulnerable learners who spend the most time with TAs are at increased risk of developing a learned helplessness. Once again, we emphasise that it is the lack of clarity about TAs' roles and purpose that is the central issue here; there is no implied criticism of TAs.

A main aim of our MITA work is to invert this. If our starting point is that the teacher is responsible for 'quality first teaching', then learning should be accessible (i.e. precisely targeted and planned) and the TA's role is to add value by supporting learners to access learning independently. TA support should encourage responsibility, scaffold key points of learning, observe performance, and feed back to the teacher. We developed a straightforward, practical scaffolding framework that schools can use to improve TAs' interactions. The scaffolding framework breaks down stages of support to encourage the greatest level of independence possible, with the TA providing 'the least help first'. There are five layers:

Layer 1. Self-scaffolding: we start from an assumption that, after explanation and modelling from the teacher, all learners should be able to attempt the task independently. Our first stage is to create opportunities for learners to problem-solve by themselves. This is an important diagnostic space in which TAs can assess whether further support is needed.

Layer 2. Prompting: the next stage is to provide positive support with virtually no information about the learning activity itself. Effective use of wait-time and open questioning (i.e. 'What do you think you need to do first?') provides positive encouragement and ensures the learner remains in control of the task.

Layer 3. Clueing: clueing provides a small piece of information relating to the area of the learning activity that the learner is struggling with. It may be a nudge to help recall a piece of information or a successful strategy to move forward. Clues are drip-fed, with each one revealing slightly more information.

Layer 4. Modelling: after moving through the layers above, the TA may need to remodel a skill or strategy that the teacher has already shared (usually via their whole-class input). Modelling should be kept short and simple, with the expectation that the learner immediately performs the same step to check understanding and demonstrate skill acquisition.

Layer 5. Correcting: this is at the bottom of our framework and should be avoided whenever possible. If TAs are doing far too much correcting, it is likely that the learner has lost control of the task.

Bringing it together

We have been fortunate to work with many hundreds of schools via our MITA programme. At its best, we see schools redefining TA roles and relationships to create a new, more expansive pedagogy, which supplements curriculum teaching with the opportunities to develop and practice metacognitive skills. By deploying TAs in ways that free up teachers, time and space are created for teachers to work with those who are struggling and deepen their understanding of their learners with SEND.

By changing their approaches to interaction, we see TAs reduce the kind of talk that tends toward task completion and create opportunities for learners to experience independence, and to develop and practise skills to manage their own learning. Breaking down patterns of separation and reliance helps schools to realise the value of TAs in delivering effective universal provision.

References and further reading

Blatchford, P., Russell, A. and Webster, R. (2012) *Reassessing the impact of teaching assistants: How research challenges practice and policy.* Oxon: Routledge.

Bosanquet, P., Radford, J. and Webster, R. (2021) *The teaching assistant's guide to effective interaction: How to maximise your practice.* Second edition. Oxon: Routledge.

Department for Education. (2019) *School workforce in England: November 2019.* Available at: www.gov.uk/government/statistics/school-workforce-in-england-november-2019 (Accessed: 30 April 2021).

Ginnis, S., Pestell, G., Mason, E. and Knibbs, S. (2018) *Newly qualified teachers: Annual survey 2017.* London: DfE. Available at: https://assets. publishing.service.gov.uk/government/uploads/system/uploads/attachment_data/file/738037/NQT_2017_survey.pdf (Accessed: 30 April 2021).

Radford, J., Blatchford, P. and Webster, R. (2011) 'Opening up and closing down: How teachers and TAs manage turn-taking, topic and repair in mathematics lessons.' *Learning and Instruction,* 21(5): pp. 625–635.

Rubie-Davies, C., Blatchford, P., Webster, R., Koutsoubou, M. and Bassett, P. (2010) 'Enhancing learning? A comparison of teacher and teaching assistant interactions with pupils.' *School Effectiveness and School Improvement,* 21(4): pp. 429–449.

Sharma, U. and Salend, S. J. (2016) 'Teaching assistants in inclusive classrooms: A systematic analysis of the international research.' *Australian Journal of Teacher Education*, 41(8). Available at: http://dx.doi.org/10.14221/ajte.2016v41n8.7 (Accessed: 30 April 2021).

Sharples, J., Webster, R. and Blatchford, P. (2018) *Making Best Use of Teaching Assistants. Guidance Report*. Second edition. London: Education Endowment Foundation. Available at: https://educationendowmentfoundation.org.uk/tools/guidance-reports/making-best-use-of-teaching-assistants/ (Accessed: 30 April 2021).

Webster, R. and Blatchford, P. (2014) 'Worlds apart? The nature and quality of the educational experiences of pupils with a Statement for special educational needs in mainstream primary schools.' *British Educational Research Journal*, 41(2): pp. 324–342.

Webster, R., Bosanquet, P., Franklin, S. and Parker, M. (2021) *Maximising the impact of teaching assistants in primary schools: A practical guide for school leaders*. Oxon: Routledge.

Webster, R., Russell, A. and Blatchford, P. (2016) *Maximising the Impact of Teaching Assistants: Guidance for school leaders and teachers*. Second edition. Oxon: Routledge.

PART 3
TARGETED PROVISION

Targeted provision is the deployment of tailored interventions or staff to support a learner's needs. In this section we draw on the expertise of authors who are (or have been) SENCOs. First, Kenny Wheeler looks at how evidence can be collected about learners' needs. Then in chapters 7 and 8 Nicole Dempsey and Cassie Young discuss the role of SENCO and the evidence for a whole-school approach to SEND provision.

6. ONE-PAGE PROFILES: CREATING YOUR OWN EVIDENCE

KENNY WHEELER

As we travel further toward targeted provision, the evidence base reduces significantly. However, SEND specialist, Kenny Wheeler, uses his chapter to suggest how teachers can create a type of ethnographic study of learners with SEND in order to facilitate learning and ensure these individuals achieve the best possible outcomes.

One-page profiles feature in many settings and act as a way of capturing what is meaningful to a young person and help outline what key staff can do to support the young person within the learning environment. In research terms, you can consider these as a one-page ethnographic study of a learner.

One-page profiles – key overview of the young person

One-page profiles are often linked to learners with SEND and used as a vehicle to find out more about the individual as part of the graduated approach. They are a great tool for capturing what is important to the young person, what they and others like about themselves, what works for them in terms of support and goals/targets that they are going to work towards. It is a vehicle to capture what is important for a young person; having this knowledge then enables adults to work with them with a better insight into the individual. They provide an opportunity to demonstrate that a setting values what is important to the young person and can act as evidence to help show the journey a young person has been on. They can be especially useful to highlight the changing circumstances some young people experience on a frequent basis.

What difference can they make?

There have not been any published studies into the efficacy or impact of one-page profiles. However, if we make reference to Herzberg's hygiene factors and motivators (1964), we might see why one-page profiles can be helpful in getting learners engaged and invested in their own learning and progress. We often look at what might motivate a young person to engage or improve at something (writing, reading, behaviour) but we also need to be aware of any barriers to engagement experienced by the young person.

The ethics of collecting information on individuals

Young people should be central to the process of creating a one-page profile. Essentially this is a document that belongs to them so it should reflect their thoughts, feelings and hope for the future. It should not be a done unto process whereby they are passive recipients who are told what they are good at and what they should be working towards in the future. They may well need support in creating a one-page profile but the content needs to authentically reflect the views and context of the young person.

If we use person-centred approaches (Sanderson et al., 2018), we can start to explore the wider context in which the young person exists. School is only a fraction of that person's life; what happens beyond the school gates may well have a significant influence on their overall wellbeing. If we can find out about the holistic young person, then we might uncover unique facts that we need to address first before looking to motivate them.

Using person-centred approaches to start to find out about the holistic young person can help identify potential triggers or factors that inhibit them from engaging within the wider learning environment. We can start exploring what might constitute a good day and what might constitute a bad day. Taking the time to find out about the individual, we start to realise that there are issues that we may not have appreciated, and which are acting as a barrier to engagement.

Good day and bad day

What does a good day actually look like for an individual? Could it be that they get breakfast on a good day, that they manage to make it to school on time, maybe they don't get bullied on the bus to school, or they have geography? There is a whole host of things we can explore with a young person that makes a day good for them. This offers a great opportunity to explore the positives they have most days.

We can then progress to look at what makes a bad day. What things happen or might happen that can turn things bad and sometimes lead to the downward spiral which results in withdrawal, outbursts or a general lack of effort in lessons. It might be that some of the things are not related to school at all but their impact means that the young person is just not in the right place to engage. Could it be they didn't sleep because of noise in the house? Maybe they had no breakfast because there is no food in the house, they got bullied on the way in to school because their uniform is ill-fitting or dirty or maybe it's because they have English which means they have to read aloud in lessons (something that they get anxious about).

Relationship circles – who features in the young person's life

While we look at good days and bad days, we can also explore relationships with the young person. Who is closest to them, who do they like and trust, who do they socialise with but perhaps do not trust and who else features in their life? From this we can create a relationship circle which highlights all the key people in their life at that point in time. If we see that a particular relative features in the middle of the relationship circle, then we make preparations if we know that there is going to be a change in family dynamics. Again, this key information can help when we are building a relationship with the young person and can help with empathic approaches if we find out that relationships are volatile in their life.

If we get this information, then we can at least start thinking about possible ways to address these issues. Maybe we can get them to check in with a member of staff each day when they arrive at school to just say how they are feeling. If they haven't had breakfast, then we can get them something to eat. If we know what the issue is, then we can do something about it. We can make reasonable adjustments so that the young person is in a better place to be ready to learn. If the young person is in receipt of Pupil Premium funding, then we could adopt a more personalised approach to their support and target spending with a better knowledge of what is likely to make a difference for the individual.

Hopes and dreams – working towards aspirations and taking action

From this point we can start exploring aspirations with the young person and talk through what they might like to do in the future. This is by no means getting a six-year-old to create a CV but more the case that we start looking at what they might be able to do given their age and what might be available to them within the community (and beyond). Potentially this is an opportunity to start showing the young person that they might be able to engage in activities that would be of interest to them but that they had not considered possible.

Once we have identified activities, potential interests or vocational routes then we can start thinking about the actions the young person, their family, the school and other stakeholders can take in order to help make the ideas more of a reality. What do we need to do to help realise one of the hopes of the young person? It could be that they join a club if they want to further an interest, perhaps joining a football club if they want to get better at football or if they wanted to widen their social circles. Alternatively, they could volunteer to support a local organisation if they wanted to develop their leadership skills and help with the development of younger peers. If the ambition is to travel to a country, then the young person might take language classes that are available in the school or in the local community so they can better understand the language and culture. Through this process, we are showing that there are possibilities that might appeal to the young person. This is not about social mobility; it is about preparing young people for life beyond the school setting. It is about showing that we do need to take some action so that we can realise our hopes for the future.

Engaging with and capturing parent/carer voice

An important part of this process is looking to gain a holistic insight into the young person's life that will also involve gaining the views and thoughts of parents/carers. Consideration needs to be given as to the best way to do this. It might be that the best way to meet and gain views from parents/carers is by meeting away from the school site. We often talk about hard-to-reach parents, but it might just be that the school environment is intimidating for some so a neutral venue might be more comfortable for them. Start with transparency by outlining the purpose behind creating a one-page profile, making it clear that the information will help you support the young person and help them to work towards mutually agreed outcomes.

There is the opportunity to use the tools outlined above along with the Preparing for Adulthood (2017) Outcomes Tool so you can explore what will help in preparing the young person for the next stage in their life. Working together will also help in ensuring that there is a consistent approach when working with the young person both at home and at school. Parents/carers can give invaluable information that will help in piecing together an accurate overview for the young person and may well provide useful strategies that staff can use in the school setting.

Meeting with parents/carers might also reveal that they themselves might benefit from additional support or further guidance. This is an opportunity to build relationships and make sure that the young person and their family have access to the things that they need.

It needs to be recognised that engaging with parents can be a challenge. In a recent research study Supporting Parents on Kids Education in Schools (SPOKES) conducted in the south-west by the Plymouth Parent Partnership, only 57% of parents attended five or more of the 10 sessions being run. However, in another EEF research project, Families and Schools Together (FAST) supported by Save the Children, parental engagement was 83% but, despite this, there was no overall impact on the progress made by their children. So, while there is evidence to suggest the positives of parental engagement, there is little to actually guide as to what can actually make a positive difference to learners and their outcomes.

Consider how you are trying to engage parents

At this point it will be worth considering how we are trying to engage with parents to encourage their involvement. Traditional methods of communication such as generic letters and emails are perhaps outdated and less likely to be responded to. For example, Matthey et al. (cited in Axford et al., 2012) found that of 3740 flyers that were sent home, only 18 parents (0.5%) responded by signing up for the programme of support. So perhaps a more personalised approach is needed in the 21st century.

Direct text messaging is comparatively lower in cost and goes directly to the parent which may increase the likelihood of their responding and engaging. In a recent EEF study (Miller et al., 2017), schools communicated with parents using text messages. The average cost (over three years) of such an approach was £6 per pupil per year. The impact of this saw absenteeism drop and additional progress made in mathematics and English (although this may have been by chance). Overall, the vast majority of parents were accepting of this approach so this could be a medium to use in the future in order to arrange meetings with parents to work on person-centred documentation.

Capturing and summarising

Through these (and other) steps, we start to find out what is actually important to the child or young person. We start to see the reality in which they exist and as professionals can then use this information when working with the young person. What started as an activity to populate a one-page profile then turns into relationship building and the gathering of key information. What we gather will not only help with current support but will also help look to the future, identifying goals and actions that we can discuss with the young person. In the process we also demonstrate to the young person that they matter, that we value them and that we want to work with them (and their family) in order to help explore and realise hopes and aspirations.

Our final one-page profile is then something that the young person (and their family) own and which better reflects what really is important to the young person. It has greater clarity in relation to knowing how the young person wants to be supported as they have had the opportunity and time to reflect on their actual circumstances, what is meaningful to them and what they actually think rather than a rushed activity to tick a box and produce something which helps neither the young person nor the school setting. While it may be difficult to quantify and measure the impact a good one-page profile has, what we can see is that when done well and in a meaningful way, we have opportunities to remove barriers and support young people to engage in education.

Using one-page profiles to support smoother transitions

One of the issues in schools is that one setting can carry out some tremendous work with a young person and their family which is then lost on transition from one setting to another. If we have one-page profiles and their accompanying documentation at the forefront during transitions, then we can prepare and then put in place arrangements that meet the actual needs of the young person rather than arrangements based simply on the perceptions or assumptions made by the receiving setting.

If staff are aware of the particular traits of an individual, then it can effectively break the cycle of 'groundhog days' every September when new staff struggle to understand the reasons behind someone's behaviours. With the one-page profile and accompanying information, all staff working with the young person can engage in an informed manner. Staff will (for example) be able to see behaviours building and will have an idea of what they can do in order to alleviate any stress or anxiety to help the young person return to a level where they are able to engage once more within the learning environment. Transition meetings between teachers can focus on the progress made by the young person over the year and not just the past six weeks.

Stopping the frustrating conversations which explain the story over and over again...

Finally, one of the frustrations experienced by families of learners with SEND is that they often feel they have to explain their story and circumstances over and over. Each new teacher they meet, each professional with whom they come into contact, they have to effectively start from scratch. If professionals and families have worked together in creating a clear one-page profile with important background information pertaining to the young person then at least there is something to share beforehand. Professionals can then gain an insight into the family and the young person before engaging with them and can then start any communication from a more informed position.

Mapping the journey

One-page profiles are a type of teacher-created evidence that shows progress over time has been made with the young person and the greater insight into their circumstances can be used to help target support to help them achieve outcomes that are meaningful to them. It is a form of evidence that belongs to the young person and their family but can help support professionals in understanding a young person and, in doing so, helps ensure reasonable adjustments are made throughout their schooling.

References and further reading

Apps, J., Christie, S., Rogers, R., Ali, Z. and Cowie, C. (2019) *Parent participation framework report for Parentkind*. Available at: https://www.parentkind.org.uk/uploads/files/1/March%202019%20Parentkind%20Parent%20Participation%20Framework%20Report2.pdf (Accessed: 6 October 2021).

Axford, N., Berry, V., Lloyd, J., Moore, D., Rogers, M., Hurst, A., Blockley, K., Durkin, H. and Minton, J. (2019) *How can schools support parents' engagement in their children's learning? Evidence from research and practice.* London: Education Endowment Foundation. Available at: https://educationendowmentfoundation.org.uk/public/files/Publications/ParentalEngagement/EEF_Parental_Engagement_Guidance_Report.pdf (Accessed: 6 October 2021).

Herzberg, F. (1964) 'The motivation-hygiene concept and problems of manpower.' *Personnel Administration*, 27(1): pp. 3–7.

Miller, S., Davison, J., Yohanis, J., Sloan, S., Gildea, A. and Thurston, A. (2017) *Texting parents: Evaluation report and executive summary July 2016.* London: EEF. Available at: https://files.eric.ed.gov/fulltext/ED581121.pdf (Accessed: 22 September 2021).

Preparing for Adulthood. (2017) *Outcomes Tool.* Available at: www.preparingforadulthood.org.uk/downloads/education-health-and-care-planning/pfa-outcomes-tool.htm (Accessed: 22 September 2021).

Rice, F., Frederickson, N., Shelton, K., McManus, C., Riglin, L. and Ng-Knight, T. (2015) *Identifying factors that predict successful and difficult transitions to secondary school.* London: Nuffield. Available at: https://nuffieldfoundation.org/wp-content/uploads/2019/11/STARS_report.pdf (Accessed: 22 September 2021).

Sanderson, H., Goodwin, G., Kinsella, E., Smith, T., Jones, V., Higgins, C., Ralphs J. and Byatt, L. (2018) *A guide to using person-centred practices in schools.* Available at: http://helensandersonassociates.co.uk/papers/using-person-centred-practices-schools/ (Accessed: 22 September 2021).

7. NO SENCO IS AN ISLAND

NICOLE DEMPSEY

Nicole Dempsey was the Individual Needs Coordinator at Dixons Trinity Academy, a secondary free school in Bradford. She is currently the Dixons Academies Trust Assistant Principal, focused on SEND, inclusion and safeguarding.

In her chapter, Nicole reviews the history and development of the SENCO Role. She then makes a clearly evidenced argument as to why the SENCO role, and potentially the whole SEND system, need urgent reform.

How can the SENCO role be best deployed to ensure the progressive inclusion and high-quality education of learners with SEND while also protecting the wellbeing of those that hold the SENCO post?

The uniqueness of the role

Without doubt, the SENCO role is unique: possibly one of the most challenging and misunderstood roles in the education sector. It remains one of only two statutory roles for a school, the other being headteacher, and it is the only one mandated to postgraduate qualification level (DCSF, 2008; DfE, 2015; Curran et al., 2018). Indeed, it may be the most legislated role a school is guaranteed to have, as SENCOs are accountable to statutes and guidance specific to them as well as those of all teachers and education practitioners. Despite this, and as will be explored in more detail in this chapter, it remains little understood, greatly varied and consistently considered – and evidenced to be – unmanageable and not functioning as intended. What is more, the entire history of the role has seen repeated review and reform and yet the educational and, where comparisons can be made, adult outcomes for our learners with SEND remain poor (Glover and Ayub, 2010; O'Brien, 2016; NHS Digital, 2018; DWP, 2019; NAO, 2019; Ryan, 2019; Dempsey, 2020). For me, although I cannot meaningfully add to the wealth of guidance – both statutory and in the form of books and websites – that is already out there, and with the early signs of the cycle of review and reform being on the horizon, I do feel that there is a need for us to step back from the noise around the role and ask ourselves, what can be done now? What can be done by us? The children in our schools now do not have time to wait. This chapter aims to reach out to SENCOs and senior leaders, but also all classroom practitioners and contributors to our school communities, to consider the current context, examine the available research and data, and then set out a way of understanding how each of us can begin to make things better for our learners with SEND regardless.

The evolution of the role

The idea of a special educational needs coordinator role in schools has been evolving since the 1980s (Cowne et al., 2019) but was first enshrined in formal guidance in the original Code of Practice on the Identification and Assessment of Special Educational Needs (DfE, 1994). What it actually says about the role is fairly minimal, just two paragraphs outlining the practical duties and acknowledging that there will be variation dependent on school context, but no hint of an early understanding of the complexity the role would prove to have (Peterson, 2010). In this first incarnation, the SENCO was guidance only and there was no requirement for them to be a qualified teacher (DfE, 1994). The realities of the role must have become apparent fairly quickly though because the evolution began early. Firstly, the introduction of the National Standards for Special Educational Needs Coordinators in 1998 (TTA, 1998) followed by an exponential increase in the amount of guidance provided specifically for the SENCO position in the 2001 version of the SEN Code of Practice (DfES, 2001), including the role now being a statutory requirement in every maintained school. There was then a flurry of concern and activity in the mid to late 2000s, culminating in the requirement for all SENCOs to have completed the postgraduate National SENCO Award qualification within three years of taking up the post, and then the New Code of Practice 0-25 years (DfE, 2015) delivering more detail and specificity to the role again. Surely this is one of the steepest trajectories any role in education has ever seen? The changes that had been made so far were thought to be progressive and conducive to improvement before the most recent reforms (Hallett and Hallett, 2010) but cracks in the veneer have been apparent throughout. The work of the House of Commons Education and Skills Committee, and subsequent developments (namely, the introduction of the National SENCO Award), were a response to concerns around the wide variation in how the role was being deployed (Education and Skills Committee, 2006) and the conversations about the untenable nature of the list of duties, as well as the issue of inconsistency despite extensive guidance, long predate the current ones (Hallett and Hallett, 2010; Norwich, 2010; Peterson, 2010; Ekins, 2012). Somehow, being a SENCO is simultaneously heavily regulated and almost completely open to interpretation. Somehow, it is both ever evolving and at a worrying standstill, with the current early indicators from various surveys and reviews showing not only that history may be about to repeat itself (Education and Skills Committee, 2019; NAO, 2019; Timpson, 2019; Ofsted, 2021) but that the 2015 reforms may have exacerbated, not improved, the situation (Sharma and Desai, 2002; Warnes et al., 2021).

The current picture for SENCOs has been brought into sharp focus by the SENCO Workload Survey and subsequent reports (Curran et al., 2018). It is difficult to read the findings and not see a system at crisis point, albeit bubbling under the surface due to lack of understanding from school leaders and colleagues. I would encourage all readers to take a look at the report for themselves – these findings have implications for us all – but some of the key statistics include:

- 59% of SENCOs felt they did not have sufficient time to meet the needs of children with an EHCP and 74% felt that way about children at the SEN Support stage.
- Only 26% of those surveyed felt the role was manageable for one person and 78% stated that they are regularly pulled away from their SENCO role by other responsibilities – only 8% said they had no other responsibilities.
- 46% of respondents felt that their role was understood by the senior leadership team (although this dropped to 26% for secondary schools) and only 27% overall felt their role was understood by colleagues.
- 71% identified administrative tasks as taking up the majority of their time, and meetings/liaisons (with parents, colleagues, other agencies, etc.) came in second place, clearly leaving less time for strategic leadership activities (ibid.).

The SENCO having a role in the strategic development of SEND policy within a school has been recognised since the second version of the Code of Practice (DfES, 2001) and so too has the debate around whether or not the SENCO should be part of a school's senior leadership team (Woodley, 2017; Murray, 2018; Cowne et al., 2019; Dempsey, 2020), despite it being recommended – not enforced – for over 20 years. Making it a point of regulation and not choice is a key recommendation of the SENCO Workforce Survey (Curran et al., 2018), but there is also recognition that its effectiveness is dependent on context (Murray, 2018), perhaps especially the expertise and experience of the SENCOs themselves, and Hallett and Hallett (2010) were already advising against thinking too much about status over intention and impact before it was reiterated in the most recent incarnation of the Code of Practice.

An update to the report in early 2020 highlights, for the most part, a lack of change i.e. the same issues being raised as before, but with the following worrying development: although 17% reported that they had been allocated more time for the role in 2019-20 compared to 2018-19, and half had stated no change at all, a concerning 22% overall had been allocated less time, and this rose to 32% in secondary schools (Curran et al., 2020a). This is particularly concerning as time, namely the manageability of the role for one person, has been a recurring theme, despite there being guidance to operate as a team in larger schools or where SEND numbers are high as far back as in the original Code of Practice (DfE, 1994). There has also been a Covid-19 specific update and, perhaps not surprisingly, the consensus is that partial school closures and the pandemic only exacerbated existing problems in the system for SENCOs and inclusion (Curran et al., 2020b). A concurrent parent survey, ran by the parent information website *Special Needs Jungle*, found that these views were echoed with great synchronicity by parents and carers of children with SEND (Moloney, 2021); particularly important as another theme of the negative discourse around the 2015 reforms is that its remit to simplify systems and co-work with families has not been met.

SENCOs in the wider educational discourse

The conversations about SEND and inclusion, including conversations about the role of SENCO, seem to exist almost entirely separately from the wider conversations about education as a whole (Dempsey, 2020). Despite the notion that all teachers are teachers of SEN (DfE, 2015) being well known across the sector, the conversations about SENCO workload and inconsistency tend to be devoid of real consideration of the roles of others within a school, or the interdependent relationship between inclusivity and whole-school culture; in essence, how the school is led (Dyson and Millward, 2000; Booth and Ainscow, 2002; Rayner, 2007; Ekins, 2010; Day et al., 2016; Garner, 2016; Bartram, 2019; Dempsey, 2020). A very recent study looking at teachers' attitudes towards inclusive education found that, against a backdrop of increasing numbers of learners with SEND in various settings, less than half of those surveyed felt that education should embody principles of equality, quality and inclusion for all (Warnes et al., 2021). The report identifies competing concepts of inclusion as being difficult to grasp for classroom teachers, inconsistent practice, and 'ambivalent' attitudes towards full inclusion i.e. all learners taught within the same classrooms as challenges for teachers, and diversity in classrooms as a cause of higher stress levels (ibid.). In light of this, as well as concerns around inequities of resource and provision (Bines, 2000) and funding cuts of 17% since 2015 for learners with SEND (Parveen, 2019), it has never, in my opinion, been more necessary for us to shift the focus of our training and support away from SEND specialists such as SENCOs and towards classroom teachers and school leaders.

Perhaps more concerning, this study is an adaptation and update of one conducted 20 years ago, just after the second version of the Code of Practice (DfES, 2001), and shows little, even no change in attitude over that period of time (Sharma and Desai, 2002; Warnes et al., 2021). In the relatively short history of the SENCO role (in comparison with the whole history of schools and education), the associated difficulties have been known throughout and, it seems, the cycle of review and reform has failed to ever fully address them. At the time of writing we are, once again, at the review stage of that cycle and the information being presented is dire (Curran et al., 2018; 2020a; 2020b; Education and Skills Committee, 2019; NAO, 2019; Timpson, 2019). With no crystal ball at my disposal, only time will tell if the inevitable changes brought about by these findings will move us forward from these recurring concerns, but what I do know is this: the children in our schools right now do not have the time to wait for us to find out.

Just as I cannot add to the wealth of guidance on the SENCO role that is already out there, nor can I add to the list of recommendations that is already available. Not only does each report come with its own list, but contemporaneous literature on the topic of inclusion in education often provides its own suggestions for ways forward. One underlying reality of the situation that we have not yet mentioned is that schools and the education system as a whole already existed long before the concept of inclusion was introduced (Slee, 2019; Dempsey, 2020; Sobel and Alston, 2021) and thus all aspects of inclusion could be seen as add-ons and annexes to that established system. Maybe what is actually needed is systemic overhaul? Do any of the recommendations we are seeing represent that? Maybe the issue we are dealing with is not one of SENCO workload, or even teacher motivation for inclusion, but of the political will to implement full inclusion or radically overhaul our priorities in relation to education (Oswald and Swart, 2011; Done, 2019; Warnes et al., 2021). With time not on our side and historical context not being promising, I ask again: what can we do now? What can we do ourselves?

Next steps for SENCOs

The information we need in order to make a start is already available. We know that the academic and related adult outcomes for those with learning disabilities are consistently poor (Glover and Ayub, 2010; O'Brien, 2016; NHS Digital, 2018; DWP, 2019; House of Commons Library, 2019; NAO, 2019; Ryan, 2019; Dempsey, 2020), that the biggest attainment gap at age 16 nationally is between learners with and without SEND (EEF, 2017) and that changes that affect in-school variation have a greater impact on national averages than changes that are aimed at between-school variation (OECD, 2004): maybe it is the outcomes of our learners with SEND that have the greatest potential to improve our schools' overall outcomes (Dempsey, 2020). We know that all teachers are teachers of SEND and that the first step and bottom line of inclusive education for learners with SEND is high-quality teaching (DfE, 2015). We know what a high-quality education looks like too because we do it every day for our learners who are not identified as SEND. We also know that it is part of the SENCO's role to take part in the strategic development of the school and to provide professional development and support to their colleagues so that learners with SEND can access the high-quality teaching that they need (DfE, 1994; 2015; DfES, 2001), and we know that most SENCOs do not feel that they have time to enact this aspect of their role and that many feel little understood by their senior teams and colleagues (Curran et al., 2018; 2020a; 2020b). It seems clear to me that, whatever our role is within our school, the keys to improving inclusivity are understanding, ownership and motivation.

So, how can the SENCO role be best deployed to ensure the progressive inclusion and high-quality education of learners with SEND while also protecting the wellbeing of those that hold the SENCO post? The bad news is that it will depend on the phase, size and location of your school, the number of learners with SEND you have on roll, the quality of your classroom teaching and universal offer, and the expertise, experience and preferences of the SENCO themselves. The good news is this; all the information we need is already out there, and there is nothing stopping us from using it.

References and further reading

Avramidis, E. and Norwich, B. (2002) 'Teachers' attitudes towards integration/inclusion: a review of literature.' *European Journal of Special Needs Education*, 17(2): pp. 129–147.

Bartram, D. (2019) *Leading great SEND provision in schools*. (14th September) Available at: https://chatterpack.net/blogs/blog/leading-great-send-provision-in-schools-by-david-bartram-obe (Accessed: 10 October 2019).

Bines, H. (2000) 'Inclusive standards? Current developments in policy for special educational needs in England and Wales.' *Oxford Review of Education*, 26(1): pp. 21–33. Available at: https://doi.org/10.1080/030549800103836

Booth, T. and Ainscow, M. (2002) *Index for inclusion: Developing learning and participation in schools*, rev. edn. Bristol: CSIE.

Cowne, E., Frankl, C. and Gerschel, L. (2019) *The SENCo handbook: Leading and managing a whole school approach*. London: Routledge.

Curran, H., Moloney, H., Heavey, A. and Boddison, A. (2018) *It's about time: The impact of SENCO workload on the professional and the school*. Available at: www.bathspa.ac.uk/media/bathspaacuk/education-/research/senco-workload/SENCOWorkloadReport-FINAL2018.pdf (Accessed: 3 July 2021).

Curran, H., Moloney, H. and Boddison, A. (2020a) *National SENCO Workforce Survey: Time to review 2018-2020*. Available at: www.bathspa.ac.uk/media/bathspaacuk/projects/National-SENCO-Workforce-Survey--Full-Report--24.06.21.pdf (Accessed: 12 September 2021).

Curran, H., Moloney, H. and Boddison, A. (2020b) *National SENCO Workforce Survey 2020*. Available at: www.bathspa.ac.uk/media/bathspaacuk/projects/15432-National-SENCO-Workforce-Survey-2020-PAGES.pdf (Accessed: 12 September 2021).

Day, C., Gu, Q. and Sammons, P. (2016) 'The impact of leadership on student outcomes: How successful school leaders use transformational and instructional strategies to make a difference.' *Educational Administration Quarterly*. 52(2): pp. 221–258.

DCSF. (2008) *21st century schools: A world class education for every child*. London: HMSO.

Dempsey, N. (2020) 'True inclusion.' In: Lock, S. (ed.) *The researchED guide to leadership*. Woodbridge: John Catt.

DfE. (1994) *Code of Practice on the identification and assessment of special educational needs*. London: The Stationery Office.

DfE. (2015) *Special educational needs and disability Code of Practice: 0-25 years*. London: DfE.

DfE. (2019) *Special educational needs in England: January 2019.* London: DfE.

DfES. (2001) *Special educational needs Code of Practice.* Nottingham: DfES Publications.

Done, E. J. (2019) 'Education governance and the responsibility to include: Teachers as a site of discursive tension.' In: Allan, J., Harwood, V. and Jørgensen, C. (eds.), *World yearbook of education 2020.* London: Routledge, pp. 113–29.

DWP. (2019) *Households below average income: An analysis of the UK income distribution: 1994/95-2018/19.* Available at: www.gov.uk/government/statistics/households-below-average-income-199495-to-201819 (Accessed: 3 July 2021).

Dyson, A. and Millward, A. (2000) Schools and special needs: Issues of innovation and inclusion. London: Paul Chapman.

Education and Skills Committee. (2006) *House of Commons Education and Skills Select Committee report on SEN.* London: The Stationery Office.

Education and Skills Committee. (2019) *School and college funding inquiry.* London: The Stationery Office.

EEF. (2017) *The attainment gap.* Available at: https://educationendowmentfoundation.org.uk/public/files/Annual_Reports/EEF_Attainment_Gap_Report_2018.pdf (Accessed: 10 October 2019).

Ekins, A. (2010) 'Developing a joined-up approach to strategic whole school processes.' In: Hallett, F. and Hallett, G. (eds.) *Transforming the role of SENCO: Achieving the National Award for SEN Coordination.* Maidenhead: Open University Press.

Ekins, A. (2012) *The changing face of special educational needs: Impact and implications for SENCOs and their schools.* Abingdon: Routledge.

Garner, P. (2016) *Final evaluation report Send review: London Leadership Strategy.* London: LLS.

Glover, G. and Ayub, M. (2010) *How people with learning disabilities die.* Available at: www.researchgate.net/publication/257984926_How_People_With_Learning_Disabilities_Die (Accessed: 3 July 2021).

Hallett, F. and Hallett, G. (2010) 'Leading Learning: the role of the SENCO.' In: Hallett, F. and Hallett, G. (eds.) *Transforming the role of SENCO: Achieving the National Award for SEN Coordination.* Maidenhead: Open University Press.

Hettiarachchi, S. and Das, A. K. (2014) 'Perceptions of "inclusion" and perceived preparedness among school teachers in Sri Lanka.' *Teaching and Teacher Education*, 43: pp. 143–53.

House of Commons Library. (2019) *People with disabilities in employment: Briefing paper.* (2nd October) Available at: https://static1.squarespace.com/static/5db02f1e0f141315ac8751cc/t/5db6a4a4c494f4106d6e9398/1572250790343/Disability+employment+gap+2019+Powell.pdf (Accessed: 10 October 2019).

Lauchlan, F. and Greig, S. (2015) 'Educational inclusion in England: origins, perspectives and current directions.' *Support for Learning*, 30(1): pp. 69–82.

Male, D. B. and Rayner, M. (2009) 'Who goes to SLD schools in England? A follow-up study.' *Educational & Child Psychology*, 26(4): pp. 19–30.

Moloney, H. (2021) *If we truly want effective SENCOs, the government must act to make it possible.* Available at: www.specialneedsjungle.com/truly-effective-sencos-government-must-act-to-make-it-possible/ (Accessed: 12 September 2021).

Murray, L. (2018) *Models for the SENCO role: context, value and intent.* Available at: https://blog.optimus-education.com/models-senco-role-context-value-and-intent (Accessed: 12 August 2021).

NAO. (2019) *Support for pupils with special educational needs and disabilities.* Available at: www.nao.org.uk/report/support-for-pupils-with-special-educational-needs-and-disabilities/ (Accessed: 3 July 2021).

NHS Digital. (2018) *Measures from the adult social care outcomes framework: England 2017-18.* Available at: https://digital.nhs.uk/data-and-information/publications/statistical/adult-social-care-outcomes-framework-ascof/archive/measures-from-the-adult-social-care-outcomes-framework-england---2017-18 (Accessed: 3 July 2021).

Norwich, B. (2010) 'What implications do changing practices and concepts have for the role of SEN Coordinator?' In Hallett, F. and Hallett, G. (eds.) *Transforming the role of SENCO: Achieving the National Award for SEN Coordination.* Maidenhead: Open University Press.

Norwich, B. (2019) Special school placement trends and the impact of academisation on provision for SEN [Video]. Paper presented at nasen live conference, July 2019, Birmingham, UK. Available at: https://vimeo.com/352238886 (Accessed: 12 September 2021).

O'Brien, J. (2016) *Don't send him in tomorrow: Shining a light on the marginalised, disenfranchised and forgotten children of today's schools.* Carmarthen: Independent Thinking Press.

OECD. (2004) *How student performance varies between schools and the role that socio-economic background plays in this.* Available at: www.oecd.org/education/school/programmeforinternationalstudentassessmentpisa/33918016.pdf (Accessed: 10 October 2019).

Ofsted. (2021) Supporting SEND. Available at: www.gov.uk/government/publications/supporting-send/supporting-send (Accessed: 12 August 2021).

Oswald, M. and Swart, E. (2011) 'Addressing South African pre-service teachers' sentiments, attitudes and concerns regarding inclusive education.' *International Journal of Disability Development and Education*, 58(4): pp. 389–403.

Parey, B. (2019) 'Understanding teachers' attitudes towards the inclusion of children with disabilities in inclusive schools using mixed methods: The case of Trinidad.' *Teaching and Teacher Education*, 83: pp. 199–211.

Parveen, N. (2019) *Funding for pupils with special educational needs drops 17%.* The Guardian. Available at: www.theguardian.com/education/2019/apr/04/funding-pupils-special-educational-needs-send-drops-north-england (Accessed: 4 May 2019).

Peterson, L. (2010) 'A national perspective on the training of SENCOs.' In: Hallett, F. and Hallett, G. (eds.) *Transforming the role of SENCO: Achieving the National Award for SEN Coordination.* Maidenhead: Open University Press.

Rayner, S. (2007) *Managing special and inclusive education.* London: Sage Publishing.

Ryan, F. (2019) *Crippled: Austerity and the demonization of disabled people.* London: Verso.

Sharma, U. and Desai, I. (2002) 'Measuring concerns about integrated education in India.' *Asia and Pacific Journal of Disability*, 5(1): pp. 2–14.

Slee, R. (2019) 'Belonging in an age of exclusion.' *International Journal of Inclusive Education*, 23(9): pp. 909–922.

Sobel, D. and Alston, S. (2021) *The inclusive classroom: A new approach to differentiation.* London: Bloomsbury.

Teacher Training Agency (1998) *National Standards for Special Educational Needs Coordinators.* London: TTA.

Timpson, E. (2019) *The Timpson Review of School Exclusion.* Available at: https://assets.publishing.service.gov.uk/government/uploads/system/uploads/attachment_data/file/807862/Timpson_review.pdf (Accessed: 12 August 2021).

Warnes, E., Done, E. and Knowler, H. (2021) 'Mainstream teachers' concerns about inclusive education for children with special educational needs and disability in England under pre-pandemic conditions.' *Journal of Research in Special Educational Needs.* Available at: https://nasenjournals.onlinelibrary.wiley.com/doi/10.1111/1471-3802.12525 (Accessed: 12 August 2021).

Weale, S. and McIntyre, N. (2018) *Special needs pupils being failed by system 'on verge of crisis'.* Available at: www.theguardian.com/education/2018/oct/22/special-needs-pupils-being-failed-by-system-on-verge-crisis (Accessed: 12 September 2021).

Woodley, H. (2017) *'SENCO: Whole school role or hidden gem?'* Available at: www.teachertoolkit.co.uk/2017/03/05/senco/ (Accessed: 12 August 2021).

8. SEND IN PRACTICE

CASSIE YOUNG

Cassie Young is a SENCO and school leader. In this personal chapter, Cassie explains the evidence-informed decisions she has made to improve SEND provision at her school as part of a school-wide transformation plan. As well as themes covered in earlier chapters such as high-quality teaching and effective deployment of teaching assistants, this also includes clear expectations about behaviour for all learners and early engagement and structured conversations with parents.

When I started at my current school, an ad hoc approach to teaching was having seriously detrimental effects on not only our learners with SEND, but all children. An evidence-informed approach led me to strip back to the fundamentals and rethink the structures in place to support learners with SEND.

Supporting the SENCO

Evidence shows that the headteacher's leadership can drastically affect the capacity of the SENCO to develop an inclusive culture within the school (Cole, 2005). Being a head of school and SENCO (supported by a strong team) has ensured that in the school there is a deep understanding and good balance between giving children with SEND a 'voice', while considering how this is achieved to the benefit of all stakeholders. However, as noted by Cole (2004; 2005) in schools with more staff, ensuring the SENCO is a prominent figure in the leadership structure has a direct influence on the inclusion of learners with SEND and is therefore an important factor in facilitating an inclusive school setting.

Auditing skills to meet provision

Mainstream schools can encounter every type of special need at any stage in a child's educational journey. This doesn't necessarily mean that the staff within the school will have the deep theoretical understanding or training base to work effectively or immediately with these learners. Therefore, a really strategic approach to CPD, sourcing high-quality training, and talking to families and previous settings are vital.

For schools with a blended team of experienced and inexperienced staff, or when forming a new team, a skills audit is a useful way to baseline the strengths and areas of stability already available within the school and give a clear overview for the staff team. We made the decision really early on that, within our setting, we would not assign teaching assistants to classes, but to learner need. This has allowed us to move support staff around according to the need of the learners and the experience of the adults.

Effective deployment of teaching assistants

As discussed in chapter 5 by Matthew Parker and Rob Webster, teaching assistants are part of universal provision and essential to support inclusive practice in mainstream schools. Knowing this and using reports such as the *Making Best Use of Teaching Assistants Guidance Report* (Sharples et al., 2015) can ensure that they can really have a greater impact on supporting identified learners.

Deploying teaching assistants according to the need of the learners and the experience of the adult has some significant benefits: it ensures that training for the supporting adults can be more focused on individual needs; it ensures those classes with a higher need have the adult/learner ratio to benefit the whole cohort; it ensures that changing circumstances can be accommodated quickly and effectively; and it means that as children get ready for transition to KS3, there are more opportunities for independence in a more fluid and staggered approach.

An example of this targeted deployment is our school-based 'Autistic Spectrum Condition (ASC) Champion'. This is a year-long training program (once-termly session over six terms) to create a highly inclusive, whole-school ASC supportive environment. One teaching assistant attends training and is an advocate for our children with an autistic spectrum condition, in addition to children who, through early identification, could have the condition. The 'champion' can then cascade, advise and support the rest of the school community with this knowledge and seek advice from the SENCO or specialist teachers who provided the training alongside working with identified children in class.

Communication is key

Communication between staff must be based on a shared ethos, mutual respect and support. To achieve this, there must be opportunities to discuss learners regularly as class teams. We refer to these discussions as 'pupil progress meetings'. They are used to facilitate this level of conversation and we ask anyone who regularly works with the identified pupils to attend the meeting six times a year. This will often also include any multi-agency staff (speech and language specialists, specialist teaching service, educational psychologists). We feel that even if their attendance isn't possible, we can feedback in an open and transparent way to benefit our children. The main class teacher will lead these meetings that are completely child-centred, focused on questions around impact of interventions, pupil voice and wellbeing, aims for the forthcoming term and anything else we need to consider to support the child with actions for the next term. Notes are shared with all parties, including parents.

Quality first teaching

Quality first teaching should be 'the offer' for all children regardless of need. In schools where the quality of teaching is an absolute priority, every child will benefit. While many characteristics have been associated with quality first teaching since its emergence in the National Strategies, three key ideas remain consistent:

1. That the teaching provided by the main classroom teacher is absolutely critical in supporting children with SEND
2. That intervention cannot replace this teaching
3. Interventions should be monitored closely and should be provided by the most qualified individual.

Not only do these principles have support in research of embedded instruction (e.g. Jimenez and Kamei, 2015) and inclusive practice more broadly (e.g. Rix et al., 2009; Jordan and McGhie-Richmond, 2014) but are also the principles of the SEND Code of Practice (2015).

High quality teaching, differentiated for individual pupils, is the first step in responding to pupils who have or may have SEN. Additional intervention and support cannot compensate for a lack of good quality teaching. Schools should regularly and carefully review the quality of teaching for all pupils, including those at risk of underachievement. This includes reviewing and, where necessary, improving, teachers' understanding of strategies to identify and support vulnerable pupils and their knowledge of the SEN most frequently encountered.

Working in a historically 'stuck' school, problems with retention and recruitment of staff and no collective vision for teaching and policy guidelines, meant that an ad hoc approach to teaching was having seriously detrimental effects not only on our learners with SEND, but all children. In a way, it was easier to remedy this rather than trying to shift an already established culture. By starting over, it made more sense to strip back to the fundamentals of decent and consistent teaching, while taking away the 70+ interventions that were going on throughout the morning sessions up until the end of the school day.

If quality first teaching is actually happening in the classroom, that is exactly where all the children should be: no compromise and no excuse. We made the decision to remove any 'out of class' interventions in the mornings, to ensure that all teachers, support staff and pupils were in class together, being utilised to meet the needs of all learners. Following this, if further support is needed, we use specifically trained individuals to take short sessions (10–40 minutes) in the afternoons for six-to-12-week periods, closely monitored by the SENCO and class teacher to ensure that it is the right strategy or intervention to use. These individuals receive high-quality training to deliver highly structured, evidence-based intervention programmes which are regularly reviewed.

Assess, plan, do, review

In response to the Code of Practice, using the graduated approach 'assess, plan, do, review' becomes a tool initially used by the class teacher to look at the needs across the class, and then plan for any individual children who need additional 'in class' support (DfE and DoH, 2015). This can be additional to or different from usual class support, followed by targeted intervention by a specialist teacher through referral, or the most skilful adult to give the extra support.

Using this approach means that we are regularly reviewing the support in place. Learner progress meetings are used to keep track of the impact of support and adjusting or changing our plans as needed. Impact is evaluated by looking at work, talking to learners and teacher assessment through low-stakes quizzing, question and answer sessions and assessment. This is used for all children on the SEND register, or at the monitoring phase of support to ensure the earliest intervention is possible. This has proved to be beneficial in many ways:

- To ensure teachers and support staff have an 'at a glance' guide to what support children are receiving in order to take ownership of the intervention

- It is used as a starting point to any parent, outside agencies or inclusion meetings
- Comprehensively building up a picture of strategies and input successes or failures
- Reduces workload long term when collating evidence if the learner is going forward for an EHCP assessment.

Behaviour

Having consistently high expectations in behaviour has got to be the fundamental base to build from to support learners with SEND. Without a clear, consistent and relentless drive to ensure the school's behaviour policy is followed by all adults and learners, the school culture can be seen as unsafe, unreliable and raising anxiety in many learners (Reaves et al., 2018). Clear routines and structures need to be carefully thought about all the time and the senior leadership team needs to lead and communicate these expectations to everyone persistently (Moore et al., 2019). With clear routines and reinforced expectations, mutual trust, reliability and safety are built upon and can thrive.

I noticed, through observation in the early days of leadership, that the learners were passive, did not respond to questions, shrugged or hid behind their hand. Our school improvement adviser said that this was an historic behaviour and hard to deal with without raising anxieties with some of our children. Furthermore, it became apparent that it could cause our most vulnerable children the biggest challenges. For example, children with autistic spectrum conditions, attachment types and children with mental health difficulties were struggling to cope with transitions, timing and lining up without a consistent routine. We found that pupils with speech and language difficulties would miss verbal instructions or directions and this would raise anxiety.

When in classroom environments, we used the work of Doug Lemov (2015) and adapted this to meet the needs of our children. I devised FUEL:

Face the speaker – this does not mean just the adults, but getting children into the habit of looking at whoever is speaking.[1]

Understand – ensuring that if pupils don't understand, or need clarification, they ask. Some of our children who find this difficult use

---

1 For clarity, for some children this is an unhelpful burden and not expected for pupils who find expressive communication overwhelming, therefore this is highlighted to the adults in the class and forms part of their one-page profile.

either a traffic light system on their tables or have adult 'check ins', to meet this expectation.

Engage and respond – this runs alongside Lemov's 'no opt out' strategy (2015). However, we decided to extend this further to provide explicit structures so that teachers could support students to 'opt in'. By modelling sentences or supporting sentence starters we believe that students can have greater confidence in answering the question, and everyone attempts to respond and engage.

Listen carefully – we talk regularly as a whole school about the fact that 'listen carefully' should be a given, if all the other steps are followed. If the pupils are facing the speaker, have clarified their understanding and are engaging and responding, then they are actively listening. Nothing is a surprise to our pupils; they know the expectations and exceed them frequently!

Using the phrase 'FUEL' is also tied in with our locality and history (site of a Royal Air Force Advanced Landing Ground, during WW2) and our school houses (Lancaster, Spitfire, Hurricane, Mustang) so we talk about pupils having 'Learning Fuel', which we feel softened the introduction of this fixed approach.

We revisit these expectations at the beginning of every term (six times a year) and any children who need support to work towards this are given the tools and strategies to meet these expectations. Individual behaviour plans that do not deviate from the policy, but may be adjusted with extra steps with adult support, or ABC (action, behaviour and consequence) to track patterns or triggers, have also been hugely effective.

Based on Marzano's levels of school effectiveness (Marzano, 2012), the real focus for us was level one: making our school a safe and orderly environment that supports cooperation and collaboration. We wanted pupils, staff and parents/carers to describe the school as a safe and orderly place, with clear plans if something went wrong. This was only achieved by having a fair, easy to follow and modelled behaviour policy, shared and consented to by the whole community. Using FUEL is an expectation for all our children and has really transformed the way in which our SEND pupils communicate both peer to peer but also peer to adult. Setting expectations and communicating them really clearly all the time, using multiple strategies such as non-verbal signs and visual prompts to support processing or language disorders, reduces anxiety or miscommunication with many children. Simply putting a routine in place alleviated many of these difficulties, but it also had wider benefits, such as cutting down the time to move around the building and low-level disruptions (deciding who was first, last and middle in a line can be a major time waster with primary-aged children!).

Parental engagement

The real change to the way in which mainstream schools work with learners with SEND is the role of parents and the learner. There is now a focus on a family-centred approach which means that schools should be working closely, communicating clearly and including the young person's wishes, aspirations and needs in what they decide and the support they give. We know from the work of Desforges (2003) and Higgins and Katsipataki (2015) that it is easier to get parents involved earlier rather than later to improve outcomes and this applies to all children, regardless of need. This was an area that had the biggest impact on the success and inclusion of learners with SEND.

Morewood and Bond (2012) write about understanding parental confidence in an inclusive school, highlighting that there is much variation in experiences of parents of learners with SEND. This work demonstrated how important a whole-school approach is but also how there needed to be a balance between following procedure and building a trusting and mutually respectful relationship with parents. The paper also mentions that feedback from a parental survey reveals that:

> the most favourably rated areas included: knowing who to contact if there was a concern; feeling listened to by the school; perceiving staff as ready to help; not feeling worried when my child is at school; and feeling my knowledge of my child is valued. (ibid.)

These are relatively easy ways to build trust and confidence. By signposting inclusion teams, making contacting staff easy and being clear with all communication, relationships can be improved quickly. Work with all parents/carers needs to be as open, honest and as sensitively handled as possible, without losing the robustness of the conversation.

Structured conversations help to establish a wider school culture of listening to the thoughts and aspirations of parents of young people with SEND. In short: 'receiving' as well as 'transmitting' information.

Originally, this was to improve the engagement of our learners with SEND and families, but we felt that this rich dialogue and interaction was something that would strengthen relationships, understanding and targeted support for all children. The conversations are based around the questions:

- What are your child's qualities and strengths?
- When are they at their best? When do they find things a challenge?
- What would you like them to do, in the short term?
- What are your long-term hopes and aspirations for your child?

The teachers add to the dialogue:

- We think your child's strengths and difficulties are…
- We think they would benefit from these targets…
- We will help you at home by supporting this…

Teachers and support staff are given time to look over this paperwork and look at how they can ensure that learner and parental wishes are incorporated in the day-to-day education of our young people. Luckily, with a strong culture of high expectation, sharing our school focus and ensuring we align our school vision and values to match the needs of all our learners, there is not much deviation from the fundamentals.

References and further reading

Bartram, D. (2018) *Great expectations: Leading an effective SEND strategy in school*. Woodbridge: John Catt Educational.

Cole, B. A. (2004) *Mother-teachers: Insights into inclusion*. London: David Fulton.

Cole, B. A. (2005) '"Good faith and effort?" Perspectives on educational inclusion.' *Disability & Society*, 20(3): pp. 331–344.

Cole, B. A. and Johnson, M. (2004) 'SENCOs and the revised Code of Practice.' Unpublished Survey, The University of Sheffield and Keele University.

Cowne, E., Frankl, C. and Gerschel, L. (2018) *The SENCo handbook: Leading and managing a whole school approach*. London: Routledge.

Desforges, C. and Abouchaar, A. (2003) *The impact of parental involvement, parental support and family education on pupil achievements and adjustment: A literature review* (Vol. 433). London: DfES.

DfE. (2015) *Special educational needs and disability code of practice: 0 to 25 years.* London: DfE.

DfE and DoH. (2015) *SEN and Disability Code of Practice: Statutory guidance for organisations who work with and support children and young people with special educational needs and disabilities.* London: HMSO.

Hayden, S. and Jordan, E. (2015) *Language for learning in the primary school: A practical guide for supporting pupils with language and communication difficulties across the curriculum.* London: Routledge.

Higgins, S. and Katsipataki, M. (2015) 'Evidence from meta-analysis about parental involvement in education which supports their children's learning.' *Journal of Children's Services,* 10(3).

Jimenez, B. A. and Kamei, A. (2015) Embedded instruction: An evaluation of evidence to inform inclusive practice. *Inclusion,* 3(3): pp. 132–144.

Jordan, A. and McGhie-Richmond, D. (2014) 'Identifying effective teaching practices in inclusive classrooms.' In: Forlin, C. and Loreman, T. (eds.) *Measuring inclusive education.* Bingley, UK: Emerald, pp. 133–162.

Lemov, D. (2015) *Teach like a champion 2.0: 62 techniques that put students on the path to college.* San Francisco, CA: Jossey-Bass.

Marzano. (2012) *Levels of school effectiveness.* Marzano Research Laboratory.

Moore, D., Benham-Clarke, S., Kenchington, R., Boyle, C., Ford, T., Hayes, R., Rogers, M. and Minton, J. (2019) *Improving behaviour in schools: Evidence review.* London: Education Endowment Foundation. The report is available from: https://educationendowmentfoundation.org.uk/education-evidence/evidence-reviews/behaviour

Morewood, G. D. and Bond, C. (2012) 'Understanding parental confidence in an inclusive high school: A pilot survey.' *Support for Learning,* 27(2): pp. 53–58.

Reaves, S., McMahon, S. D., Duffy, S. N. and Ruiz, L. (2018) 'The test of time: A meta-analytic review of the relation between school climate and problem behavior.' *Aggression and Violent Behavior,* 39: pp. 100–108.

Rix, J., Hall, K., Nind, M., Sheehy, K. and Wearmouth, J. (2009) 'What pedagogical approaches can effectively include children with special educational needs in mainstream classrooms? A systematic literature review.' *Support for Learning,* 24(2): pp. 86–94.

Ryan, W. and Gilbert, I. (2008) *Leadership with a moral purpose: Turning your school inside out*. Carmarthen: Crown House Publishing.

Sharples, J., Webster, R. and Blatchford, P. (2015) *Making best use of teaching assistants: Guidance report*. London: Education Endowment Foundation.

PART 4
SPECIALIST PROVISION

This section looks at the research evidence beyond SEND provision in mainstream schools. In chapter 9, Sabrina Hobbs discusses whether the education evidence base is strong enough (and appropriate enough) to use in special schools, a theme also picked up by Barney Angliss in chapter 10. The final chapter of the book looks at alternative provision, the prevalence of SEND within this sector and some of the reasons why this might be the case.

9. EVIDENCE-INFORMED SPECIAL SCHOOLS: DO WE HAVE ENOUGH EVIDENCE?

SABRINA HOBBS

Sabrina Hobbs was principal of Severndale Specialist Academy, one of the largest special schools in England. I set her the question of whether the educational evidence base is strong enough to support teaching and learning in special schools and I am deeply impressed by the chapter that she has written in response. While the limited number of references in the chapter may suggest that evidence is lacking, Sabrina has exemplified that evidence is only useful when it can be roundly utilised in the setting in which you work and with the learners you support. From this perspective, Sabrina explains that she has all the evidence that she feels necessary.

You would be forgiven for assuming that there is not enough evidence out there for special schools to be informed by; data sets are usually small and diagnosis-led – focusing on ASD, ADHD, etc – all of which tends not to fit the population as a whole, or ethos of a school. Examples from Severndale Specialist Academy illustrate that if we agree and align our purpose and criteria of what is meant by a school's 'success', the question of evidence is completely reframed.

Context to the discussion

To understand how evidence can inform school practice, we first need to understand the context and make-up of the school. Once this is understood, we can identify the challenges and gaps in provision, and seek out the solutions. We know that every school is different, however the exception of a special school is how its variability differs to mainstream. Its very existence relies upon what cannot be provided from the community of mainstream schools in a given area. In turn, this variable relies on the demographics of the general population, balanced with the socioeconomic context, culture, and willingness to be inclusive within that location. It may seem out of scope to identify these parameters when discussing the amount of evidence around to support special schools, however they are important factors needed to understand the reasons for such variance across this sector, and therefore the perceived lack of reliable evidence.

This chapter will review the need to collect evidence in schools and reflect on what is relative and relevant when informing special school practice. The focus of evidence-informed provision must reflect on the criteria we are using to reach a specific outcome. What do we want schools to achieve? How do special schools fit into that model? What information will tell us that we are progressing towards that goal?

Collections of evidence – what do we value?

As a society we have begun to skew our perceptions of success and what we value from our schools. We have become obsessed with exam data. Perversely, this has become the hard evidence that has ratified the success of a learner, the success of a teacher, the success of leadership, and ultimately the success of a school. This has accounted for much of the formal and informal 'league table' climates felt in the current education system; pitching children, leaders and schools up against each other in their quest to be the 'best'. This is a topic for another discussion, however it frames the problem for those schools who have very few learners, if any, who are able to 'succeed' in this way. As a result, these schools, namely special, lack the data sets and/or evidence to show these traditional measures of 'success'.

Reflecting on this situation, there is scope to scrutinise the integrity of evidencing progress and success using exam data. Does academic attainment really equate to how successful a person will be in adulthood? The answer is a resounding 'no' within the specialist sector (and possibly in the mainstream sector also!). So while the government continues to measure, collect and compare datasets to evidence progress, improvement and quality, the quest for relevant, standardised, tangible evidence continues on for special schools who are essentially excluded from this success criteria.

For the first time in the history of Severndale, summer 2019 finds us submitting our first cohort of key stage 1 and key stage 2 national assessments (SATs) and for a number of years we have also had a small number of pupils complete GCSEs. These achievements are personal to those individuals but bear no reflection on the other 95% of the school cohort who cannot attain these levels. Rather, this only serves to celebrate the attainment of individuals and to confirm changes to the ability of the pupil population.

The challenge of Severndale is its size and diversity of need: with over 400 pupils (approximately two to three times the size of an average special school), spanning three different locations, involving the whole spectrum of special needs, and full age range. There is a need to balance differences of cohorts with the need for a consistent approach. Consistency is what enables fairness and transparency to exist. It is this understanding that has driven us to identify the key principles to drive a universal approach to achieving success. This is what we value as this is what will secure positive destinations for all, regardless of ability or special needs.

Severndale's principles of success

If the purpose of education is to shape our next generation and develop a society that functions as well as it can, then identifying the qualities of what makes a person successful is key to identifying our success criteria. What these people have in common is not a set of exam results; it is the support that they have experienced, plus the high levels of participation and contribution to a cause, that they have put in.

The combination of these conditions and behaviours is what we believe schools need to foster. Tracking back from this goal, we have identified three key principles that constitute success:

1. Attendance – the routine of getting up, contributing and learning new things.

2. Parental engagement – it is 'parent-like' engagement that often provides the motivation to improve and do well. Parents/carers can better influence, model and scaffold support if they are part of the journey through school.

3. Behaviour for learning – engagement is reflected in behaviour so we can learn and build on what works, and what doesn't. Reflecting on behaviour is an essential aid to self-regulation, self-promotion and wellbeing.

These principles underpin all key aspects of teaching and learning, resource management, staffing, pedagogy, timetables, class groups and curriculum.

Collecting evidence

Data collected from our three principles is tangible, regulated and verified. Data is also relevant for all our pupils and can be compared against any other school.

Once these were established, opportunities for meaningful evidence collection opened up, empowering staff to conduct their own research to inform practice.

Staff have used these principles to shape their curiosity to measure behaviours of all stakeholders, informing strategies to drive up outcomes of increased attendance, parental engagement to events and reviews, and an improvement in pupil behaviour.

Evidence born from strands of research from our staff this year includes:

- Bullying, negative peer-to-peer behaviour, and the cognitive ability to intentionally cause harm
- Total communication in the Early Years Foundation Stage – person-centred approaches for meaning and purpose
- Complex Learning Difficulties and Disabilities in the community – recognition of visual cues in relation to environmental experiences
- Transition to mainstream – partnerships to achieve better outcomes.

Although each strand is different to the next, they all provide evidence towards our principles and will inform provision, policy and approach for how home and school can best support pupils as partners.

Do we have enough?

At Severndale, evidence is the outcome of active research that informs our understanding of not just our pupils and their attainment, but of all the stakeholders involved to ensure success beyond the school gates. Staff are encouraged to seek out solutions to overcome challenges our pupils and their families face and to deliberate alternative perspectives. We do not rely on opinion or accept limitations set by a pupil's condition. We collect evidence to aid understanding to inform decision making for our own, unique, special school context and further support our aspirations for improved future outcomes.

Our key principles capture hard data to reference relevant progress against. These create purpose and a strong sense of responsibility to ensure we continue to develop the conditions and climate for all pupils to achieve their full potential. This focus anchors a variety of research streams that enriches our evidence base in many meaningful ways.

If we look to external sources of evidence to solve internal issues, there will never be enough to fully inform our practice. Special schools are so varied and completely different to one another that the difference between schools, cohorts and locality often outweighs the relevance of what is available. Reflective, introspective practice (with an eye on the external) is therefore central to capturing learning to build upon, relying on your own school's values, purpose and principles to shape the scope and quantity of SEND evidence to utilise and be informed by.

References and further reading

Michelle Haywood (ed.) (2019) *ResearchSEND in ordinary classrooms.* Woodbridge: John Catt.

Whole School SEND. SEND gateway: Resources and Publications. Available at: www.sendgateway.org.uk/resources (Accessed 30 June 2021).

10. SINGLE, SEPARATE AND SURPRISING SOULS: THE PAST, PRESENT AND FUTURE ROLE OF RESEARCH IN SEND

BARNEY ANGLISS

Barney Angliss is a consultant, trainer, writer and researcher in SEND. When I asked Barney to write this chapter, he responded that many people will be surprised by his contribution as he uses his chapter to call on readers to consider beyond the typical 'gold standard' research methods. He invites the reader to instead consider the 'science of one' method more akin to anthropological approaches than scientific trials, but with the potential for far-reaching impact nonetheless.

'She would be a fool who tried to demonstrate the uselessness of what she knew, for there is nothing that cannot be useful if by that we mean putting knowledge to human ends.' (Marilyn Strathern, Measures of Usefulness: A diatribe.)

The creation of a deficit model

Whose is the template of the special needs child? Is it in a drawer at the Department for Education? Is it in a Convention or a Declaration? Or is it in Emily Perl Kingsley's *Welcome to Holland*? Is it the shape of our bodies or the configuration of our services?

It's frustrating that research in this field presents with even greater limitations than does the broad body of education research as a whole. Diversity of needs and practice seem to confound professional learning while inconsistency impedes the process of 'scaling' innovation. The available data – the shared knowledge of 'what works' for learners with special needs – is hampered by methodological issues, political indifference, ideological agendas and commercial disincentives.

All of this serves to reinforce the 'deficit' (medical) model of disability which has characterised special needs policy in England to no one's satisfaction: some say, 'We don't want this pathologising, ableist dogma!' while others murmur, 'We don't believe these diagnoses anyway.' Denzin (2013) reminds us: 'Objective reality can never be captured. We only know a thing through its representations.'

SEND is trapped within its medico-legal context and it often seems that the only way for young people with SEND – or their parents and carers, advocating – to gain some kind of purchase on education's craggy slopes is to characterise themselves as 'impaired', somehow less; and young people who need 'specialist' education are implicitly much *more* impaired, much *less* ideal or complete. Young people are required first to identify and second to disable themselves by statute and, most often, by diagnosis in order to receive the education they need. As Tremain (2006) observed:

> *Impairment has been disability all along ... the category of impairment emerged and in part persists in order to legitimize the disciplinary practices that it generated in the first place.*

We have failed as yet to secure quality education as a universal right without recourse to medicine and law. Nor can we yet say there is consensus on what should be provided, even assuming these punishing sacrifices of identity and autonomy could be waived. If there is a determination now to raise the profile of research in SEND above the bartering which goes on at County Hall, to settle on 'what works' rather than 'who's paying', then the researchED movement has its part to play.

Methodological limitations

Rakap (2015) highlights a particular problem: single-subject experimental research (SSER) is a common method in special education but such studies 'are often excluded from meta-analyses of evidence-based practices due to the lack of methodological consensus on the type of effect size indices to be used to determine treatment effect'. Thus it was, perhaps, that when Ofsted published its own index of educational research in 2019 the inspectorate selected 321 studies without including any whose primary focus is SEND. This is not good enough: as Jasanoff (2004) bluntly puts it:

> *Whether through direct participation or through organized questioning, the public has both a right and a duty to ask experts and their governmental sponsors whether appropriate knowledge is being deployed in the service of desired ends.*

Randomised control trials, held as the gold standard in educational research, are more difficult in SEND for several reasons: the heterogeneity of SEND makes it harder to identify enough learners for the sample; harder, too, to create control groups in a matched environment. Sadly, learners with SEND are more likely to change schools mid-phase, meaning small-group studies get even smaller; and learners in a special school may turn out to have fewer characteristics in common than expected, due to Local Authority placement practices.

Many types of SEND are 'low incidence', meaning researchers may struggle to find enough subjects; and because controversy surrounds so much in SEND that needs to be researched, their participation cannot be assured – many young people with SEND and their parents/carers have survey fatigue: they've been asked by professionals to 'tell their story' and 'give their feedback' too often and frequently only as a tick box PR exercise. Recently I was asked to help recruit subjects for a study which I found could only be done by connecting with people in closed Facebook groups, one after another, until parents hesitantly came forward whose children met the criteria. With a sense of irony, I blogged some years ago about my own experience of taking part in medical research as a child and titled the piece '$n = 1$' which, realistically, is often the case in SEND research, no matter what they tell you in the abstract.

Even assuming subjects can be assembled, how valid is the sample? What – or who – are we researching when we research SEND? It is demonstrably true and has been for many years that the incidence of special educational needs reported by schools, local authorities and the Department for Education involves precious little science, no input from disabled learners themselves and is an embarrassment to logic. It is a clumsy administrative fudge in which the outcomes of costly intervention are scarcely understood and rarely evident. The fact is that mainstream schools in England choose which pupils are on their SEND register at the initial stage (SEN Support) with almost no comparability or accountability and they don't do it well, according to the Education Policy Institute:

> ... which primary school a child attends makes more difference to their chances of being identified with SEND than anything about them as an individual, their experiences or what local authority they live in. The lottery is mostly at school level, with more than half of the differences in identification explained by the school attended. This is most unusual in education research and in stark contrast to school attainment, where between-school differences explain only a small minority of the differences in pupil test results (Hutchinson, 2021).

Besides the obvious detriment to children with special needs who are not identified when they should be, a consequence of this lottery is that large-scale research into how well children's needs are met by support arrangements is likely to be of poor quality because there is no integrity to the system for identifying them, discouraging researchers from attempting to examine the value of particular interventions and weakening advocacy.

The deeper challenge to SEND is philosophical.

The proliferation of meaningless terms to categorise children

It doesn't help that, during the 40 years since the Warnock Commission Report that preceded the first 'special needs' legislation in the UK and that the late Baroness Warnock herself later described as *'the last gasp of welfarism, struggling to survive against the pitiless advance of cost-benefit, or economic realism, which began with Thatcher, and has found its true flourishing in our new Health, Welfare and Legal Aid legislation'* (Warnock, 2018), policy-makers have been satisfied with meaningless terms to categorise children and, as a consequence, a search of the literature is a journey through gibberish. For political convenience, we are forced to swallow the nonsensical labels by which children are stereotyped whom we – teachers, parents, researchers, therapists – ought to consider only as single, separate and surprising souls.

The most obvious and depressing example of this is the widely-used classification 'moderate learning difficulties', defined by the DfE (then, the DfES) only by attainments and the type of educational provision and paperwork the child receives (DfES, 2003), a fine example of the type of government 'supplyism' which haunts SEND and that tells us precisely nothing evidence-based about what the child will need. For a pretty thorough take-down of the concept, see Norwich et al. (2014).

Norwich and Eaton (2015) found evidence that children and young people with SEND are marginalised by the system designed to support them in another way too: the focus of multi-agency meetings deflected often onto the multi-agency structure itself and away from improved outcomes for those young people, exemplifying Martin Vogel's (2018) paraphrase of Conquest's Law:

> ... *any organisation that survives long enough ends up being run in such a way as to contradict its founding purpose. As an organisation grows and becomes more complex, it ends up acting primarily to ensure its own*

perpetuation. The purpose for which it was founded becomes secondary to its own survival.

Evidence of the damage done by such organisations, whose survival depends on the crude labelling of individuals, is not merely anecdotal: it is documented in the Lenehan Review (2017), commissioned by the Department of Health, and the Confidential Inquiry into premature deaths of people with learning disabilities (CIPOLD) study (Heslop et al., 2013) published by the Norah Fry Research Centre at Bristol University. The latter found that 43% of the deaths of people with learning disabilities were unexpected, similar to the general population, but that fewer deaths of people with learning disabilities (38%) were reported to the coroner compared with the general population (46%).

CIPOLD also found that the most common reasons for deaths among people with learning disabilities being assessed as premature were: 'delays or problems with diagnosis or treatment; and problems with identifying needs and providing appropriate care in response to changing needs'. When one considers that these are the very same issues which led so many parents through the school-based SEND system and often to the SEND Tribunal, highlighted by Hutchinson (above), it becomes bleakly apparent that SEND research is vital to improve the accuracy with which needs are identified and the efficacy with which they are met.

In their sample, CIPOLD found that: 'the cause of a person's learning disability was unknown for over half (56%) of the 247 adults and children with learning disabilities who died.' I say again with sadness, labels such as severe and moderate learning difficulties do not serve our children well because they set the precedent for these children to be lost from view – and care – as adults. As O'Brien (2018) contends:

For those on the margins of mass education systems a quest for categorisation and labelling still exists - as does the vagueness of labels, especially in establishing what they really mean in educational contexts ... At a conceptual level labels about learning need highlight the perceived typicality of a group but they do not illuminate individual difference and disposition within a group. In terms of understanding individuality, labels are more about navigation than destination.

Daniels et al. (2019) argue that the history of SEND in England 'is littered with contradictions and tensions between incentives of social control and humanitarian progress', offering further evidence from Hodkinson and Burch

(2017) that the SEND Code of Practice (DfE, 2015) 'contains, constrains and constructs privilege as well as dispossession through enforcing marginality and exclusion'.

The challenge for educational research

It is for all these reasons that research conducted within the socially constructed field of SEND is of profound importance and yet excruciatingly difficult and contentious. Berliner (2002) approaches the problem imposed by a false dichotomy between hard and soft science (both of which I suggest are disputed in SEND) by breaking down the challenge of educational research into three parts.

Firstly, there is the power of educational contexts that cannot be sufficiently controlled to produce sound quantitative research, to which I previously referred. Secondly, there are the confounds of the classroom ('the ubiquity of interactions') such as the teacher's training, conceptions of learning and beliefs about assessment. Berliner (2002) cites a study of learners' evaluation anxiety in elementary and middle school classrooms which, at first glance, indicated that achievement was inversely proportional to anxiety. However, the reality was much more complex:

In some classes students' evaluation anxiety was so debilitating that their achievement was drastically lowered, while in other classes the effects were non-existent. And in a few classes the evaluation anxiety apparently was turned into some productive motivational force and resulted in improved student achievement.

In relation specifically to SEND research, variations in learners' responses under specific conditions are no more homogenous than in Berliner's example and it's likely much less due to co-morbidities and the impact of their personal histories, multiple interventions, changes in educational setting and so on.

Berliner's third obstacle is framed as the interaction of 'decade by findings' through which he suggests that:

Changes in conceptions of the competency of young children and the nature of their minds resulted in a constructivist paradigm of learning replacing a behavioural one, making irrelevant entire journals of scientific behavioural findings about educational phenomena (ibid.).

In the field of SEND teaching this is abundantly clear. Pedagogy has been overwhelmingly constructivist and progressive (characterised by the emphasis on 'differentiation' and, fairly or unfairly, by a perceived reliance on 'worksheets'). With the exception of some practice in the teaching of phonics, we are only now seeing a grassroots interest in the application to SEND of more traditionalist approaches allied with elements of cognitive science, of which this publication is a signal. In a phrase that I think speaks directly to the experience in SEND, Berliner writes:

In education, broad theories and ecological generalisations often fail because they cannot incorporate the enormous number or determine the power of the contexts within which human beings find themselves (ibid.).

To put it as politely as I can, that is what makes parents of children and young people with SEND so very angry at times: theories and percentages and blanket policies seem to mean very little from the moment when your child's life journey is revealed to be atypical and, for some, very short. It isn't that data has no value in SEND – but whose data? As a parent of a child with SEND, @StarlightMcKenzie (2019), puts it:

If we can accept both that all behaviour communicates, but that there will be a level of interpretation there, then we do have an insight into internal worlds. No science is pure, but science isn't what I am arguing for, just individualised-data-driven-evidence-based-practice.

So we need a research paradigm that does not lose sight of individual experience in the face of Berliner's three powers of context, interaction and time.

The science of one

At the head of this chapter I quoted Marilyn Strathern, an anthropologist, speaking about putting knowledge to human ends. She could equally be speaking of SEND research rather than anthropology and she could so easily be referring to Rhonda Faragher and Barbara Clarke's excellent volume bringing together evidence and experience, *Educating Learners with Down Syndrome* (2014), when she adds:

Now if the end (aim/objective) of the exercise is some enlarged capacity – and I mean conceptual rather than mental capacity – then so may be the means. That is, one expands the mind by expanding the mind, a means educationalists once called learning for its own sake.

My view here is that everyone can gain by reading specialist SEND research such as Faragher and Clarke's because it reveals fundamental qualities of human experience and educational opportunities for a population seen by many as under threat. The pressure on the Down's Syndrome population, with around 750 live births annually in the UK, is reflected in Sally Phillips's 2016 documentary, *A World Without Down's Syndrome?* (Dragonfly Film and TV, shown by the BBC) and by the campaign *Don't Screen Us Out* (www. dontscreenusout.org). It illustrates that, when it comes to research-informed policy, numbers matter because research draws its power from numbers and, indeed, seldom finds funding without them. Minorities are displaced, a risk that any society runs in placing exclusive reliance on 'evidence-based practice'. Scalability is the watchword in EBP but it serves less well in SEND.

An example of this 'science of one' which offers unique insight that *expands the mind*, as Strathern might have it, is Elly Chapple's account (2019) of her deafblind daughter teaching herself, delivered by Elly in talks around the country and published by *Special Needs Jungle*:

> *I remember clearly when I watched Ella for a period of nine months repetitively work her way through the box of shoes at our front door ... mouthing and feeling every single one ... The team and I knew that she was doing what she needed to. That without eyes, her hands had to work out every inch of every shoe and categorise that so by light touch she would know what we saw with our eyes in seconds – shoe, shoe, shoe, shoe ... After nine months, one day she simply put the last shoe down, turned from the box and stood up. She sat down in her chair and promptly said 'boots' and indicated to her foot ... The 'shoeness of a shoe' was complete.*

I have described research from different perspectives including that of specialists, of parents and, in the case of Ella with her shoes, the child conducting research into her own learning. Davina Jones and colleagues at National Star (2018) describe how Rich, an advocate and a person with disabilities, felt that his own experience helped him to engage with current students at his former college:

> *As a researcher it has added a beneficial dynamic because I am impaired and I have studied at National Star; people are able to relate to me and I understand hearing some of the stories. I am able to relate to that as something I went through.*

Similarly, Melanie Nind (2013) observes in an article for the invaluable website *PMLD Link* that 'ultimately research is about whose knowledge counts'. Nind explains:

The decision to include a group of academic researchers who do research in which they seek to maximise the participation of people with learning disabilities was in part about anticipating this and ensuring that research with people with profound impairment was represented. In the focus groups I asked:

- *Can everyone be a researcher?*
- *Can everyone give research data?*
- *What do you need to be a researcher?*
- *Has anyone done research involving people with profound and multiple disabilities?*
- *What were you trying to find out?*
- *How did you go about it?*

The question of who can do research led to answers that were grounded more in politics than experience.

I think Nind captures the tension which surrounds research that traces disability in education: not so much the research itself but its reception – the prominence afforded it – is infernally politicised so that experience is often discounted as subjective and unverifiable. The danger is that research in the hands of those best-placed to interpret and expand upon what they find, research that illuminates individual experiences of education, loses power in the larger, statistical context. The challenge is firstly to know about it, then to mine it and disseminate it, or we will forever rehearse the inclusion-location debate and let slip so much hard-won knowledge.

Science of one, theory of many?

And yet, as much as we need to embrace unique perspectives, unless we are to view research only in the sense of a kind of journalism, there must also be theory, a rationale by which we integrate research into practice and weave tightly the fabric of our knowledge. As MacLure (2010) puts it:

Theory stops us from forgetting, then, that the world is not laid out in plain view before our eyes, or coyly disposed to yield its secrets to our penetrating analyses ... It stops us from thinking that things speak for themselves – 'the data', 'practice', the pure voice of the previously silenced. It blocks our fantasies about the legibility of others – the idea that we can read other people's minds or motives. It stops us from forcing 'the subjects' out into the open where anyone and no-one can see them.

There must be discipline, a theoretical framework, in the way we use research to develop education for learners with different needs, or we can't have confidence in any of it; but it cannot be simply the discipline of numbers – I've shown that this won't work – and we should treat with caution the conclusions of systematic reviews which bleach out the useful differences and entirely lose the *shoeness* of a shoe.

References and further reading

Berliner, D. C. (2002) 'Educational research: The hardest science of all.' *Educational Researcher*, 31(8): pp. 18–20.

Chapple, E. (2019) *The deafblind world: The shoeness of a shoe*. Available at: www.specialneedsjungle.com/the-deafblind-world-the-shoeness-of-a-shoe/ (Accessed: 6 July 2021).

Cole, T. (1990) 'The history of special education: Social control or humanitarian progress?' *British Journal of Special Education*, 17(3): pp. 101–107.

Curran, T. (2013) 'Disabled children's childhood studies: Alternative relations and forms of authority?' In Curran, T. and Runswick-Cole, K. (eds.) *Disabled children's childhood studies*. London: Palgrave Macmillan.

Daniels, H., Thompson, I. and Tawell, A. (2019) 'After Warnock: The effects of perverse incentives in policies in England for students with special educational needs.' *Frontiers in Education*, 4(36).

Davis, L. J. (ed.) (2006) *The disability studies reader*. 2nd ed. New York and Abingdon: Taylor & Francis, pp. 185–197.

Denzin, N. K. (2013) 'Triangulation 2.0.' *Journal of Mixed Methods Research*, 6(2): pp. 80–88.

DfE. (2010) *The importance of teaching: The schools white paper*. London: DfE.

DfE. (2015) *Special educational needs and disability code of practice: 0 to 25 years*. London: DfE.

DfES. (2003) *Data collection by type of special educational needs*. London: DfES.

Heslop, P., Blair, P., Fleming, P., Hoghton, M., Marriott, A. and Russ, L. (2013) *Confidential Inquiry into premature deaths of people with learning disabilities (CIPOLD)*. Norah Fry Research Centre: University of Bristol.

Hodkinson, A. and Burch, L. (2017) 'The 2014 special educational needs and disability code of practice: Old ideology into new policy contexts?' *Journal of Education Policy*, 34(2): pp. 155–173.

Hutchinson, J. (2021) *Identifying pupils with special educational needs and disabilities*. EPI. Available at: https://epi.org.uk/publications-and-research/identifying-send/ (Accessed: 8 October 2021).

Jasanoff, S. (2004) 'The idiom of co-production.' In: Jasanoff, S. (ed.) *States of knowledge: The co-production of science and the social order*. London: Routledge.

Jones, D., Sweet, M., Amos, R., Faux, F. and Rozsahegyi, T. (2018) *Look inside my life*. Ullenwood: National Star College.

Kingsley, E. P. (1987) Welcome to Holland. Available at: www.emilyperlkingsley.com/welcome-to-holland (Accessed: 11 October 2021).

Lenehan, Dame C. (2017) *These are our children: A review*. Council for Disabled Children (commissioned by the Department of Health), National Children's Bureau. Available at: https://assets.publishing.service.gov.uk/government/uploads/system/uploads/attachment_data/file/585376/Lenehan_Review_Report.pdf (Accessed: 18 October 2021).

Leckie, G. and Goldstein, H. (2017) 'The evolution of school league tables in England 1992–2016: "Contextual value-added", "expected progress" and "progress 8".' *British Educational Research Journal*, 43(2): pp. 193–212.

MacLure, M. (2010) 'The offence of theory.' *Journal of Education Policy*, 25(2): pp. 277–286.

Nind, M. (2013) *Inclusive research: Where does it leave people with PMLD?* PMLD Link Journal. Available at: www.pmldlink.org.uk (Accessed: 11 October 2021).

Norwich, B. and Eaton, A. (2015) 'The new special educational needs (SEN) legislation in England and implications for services for children and young people with social, emotional and behavioural difficulties.' *Emotional and Behavioural Difficulties*, 20(2): pp. 117–132.

Norwich, B., Ylonen, A. and Gwernan-Jones, R. (2014) 'Moderate learning difficulties: Searching for clarity and understanding.' *Research Papers in Education*, 29(1): pp. 1–19.

O'Brien, T. (2018) Reflections on 'Schools: An Evolutionary View'. In *The Warnock Report 40 Years On* (virtual issue), Support for Learning, NASEN/Wiley. Available at: https://nasenjournals.onlinelibrary.wiley.com/pb-assets/assets/14679604/3.%20TIM%20O'BRIEN.pdf (Accessed: 18 October 2021).

Ofsted. (2010) *The special educational needs and disability review: A statement is not enough.* Available at: https://assets.publishing.service.gov. uk/government/uploads/system/uploads/attachment_data/file/413814/ Special_education_needs_and_disability_review.pdf (Accessed: 18 October 2021).

Ofsted. (2019) *Education inspection framework overview of research.* Available at: https://assets.publishing.service.gov.uk/government/uploads/ system/uploads/attachment_data/file/963625/Research_for_EIF_ framework_updated_references_22_Feb_2021.pdf (Accessed: 11 October 2021).

Rakap, S. (2015) 'Effect sizes as result interpretation aids in single-subject experimental research: description and application of four nonoverlap methods.' *British Journal of Special Education,* 42(1): pp. 11–33.

StarlightMcKenzie (2019) Available at: https://twitter.com/ StarlightMcKenz/status/1145322504447307776 (Accessed: 11 October 2021).

Strathern, M. (2005) 'Useful Knowledge.' Isaiah Berlin Lecture delivered at The British Academy, 2 December 2005. In: Marshall, P. J. (ed.) *Proceedings of the British Academy, Volume 139, 2005 Lectures,* published to British Academy Scholarship Online, January 2012.

Tremain, R. (2006) 'On the government of disability: Foucault, power and the subject of impairment.' In: L. J. Davis (ed.) *The disability studies reader.* 2nd ed. New York and Abingdon: Taylor & Francis, pp. 185-197, quoted in Curran, T. (2013) 'Disabled children's childhood studies: Alternative relations and forms of authority?' In: Curran, T. and Runswick-Cole, K. (eds.) *Disabled children's childhood studies.* London: Palgrave Macmillan.

Vogel, M. (2018) *Tracking down Conquest's law on organisations.* Available at: https://vogelwakefield.com/2018/12/tracking-down-conquests-law-on-organisations/ (Accessed: 6 July 2021).

Warnock, M. (2018) SEN: The past and the future. In *The Warnock Report 40 Years On* (virtual issue), Support for Learning, NASEN/Wiley. Available at: https://nasenjournals.onlinelibrary.wiley.com/pb-assets/ assets/14679604/1.%20WARNOCK-1540389396170.pdf (Accessed: 18 October 2021).

11. ALTERNATIVE PROVISION AND SEND

CATH MURRAY

Cath Murray is Chief Development Officer at Right To Succeed and prior to that was the Alternative Provision Lead at the Centre for Social Justice and a journalist at Schools Week and FE Week. Primarily drawing on DfE datasets analysed in 2019, Cath draws out startling relationships between SEND and alternative provision in England focusing in on the case of learners with social, emotional and mental health needs.

Every year alternative provision educates thousands of children with the poorest academic and life outcomes. Less than 2% achieve good passes in English and maths; half are immediately not in education, employment or training after leaving. So why are more people not asking...What is the link between alternative provision and SEND?

What is alternative provision currently used for?

Before we get into the detail, let's look at what alternative provision (AP) is, and what it is used for.

There are over 42,000 children currently registered as sole educated in AP, compared to 125,000 in special schools and eight million in mainstream. In addition, around 10,000 are dual-rolled in mainstream and AP (DfE, 2019).

One government-commissioned research paper (IFF, 2018) defines AP as:

education for pupils who, because of exclusion, illness or other reasons, would not otherwise receive suitable education; education arranged by schools for pupils on fixed-term exclusion; and pupils being directed by schools to off-site provision to improve their behaviour.

The 'other reasons' part of that statement is rather vague, but a recent market analysis of AP – also published by the DfE – collected more specific data on what AP is actually used for. Analysing responses from 118 local authorities, Isos

Partnership (2018) found that reasons include early, preventative support (78% of LAs selected this option), alternative pathways for engagement (69%), reintegrating pupils into schools (56%), new arrivals to the area (53%), and pupils off-rolled due to attendance (13%) or academic issues (12%). Interestingly for the topic we are looking at here, 52% of LAs reported using AP due to a lack of other specialist provision.

It is immediately obvious from the heterogeneous nature of these responses, that what AP should look like is not a simple question. In fact, there is an unresolved ideological debate about whether AP should be considered a place where learners who are not coping in mainstream schools receive a full-time, long-term education; whether its main function should be to offer preventative support to mainstream schools (with every child remaining on the roll of a mainstream school at all times); whether it should be a place where learners are immediately assessed and triaged into suitable specialist or mainstream schools; or a mixture of all of the above.

For the sake of statistics, AP establishments are divided into two groups. The first contains those included in the termly school census: pupil referral units (PRUs), AP converter academies (often former PRUs) and AP free schools. Roughly speaking, these tend to be where learners are sent after permanent exclusion or if they arrive in the local authority without a school place. For ease of comprehension, we shall refer to these three types of school collectively as 'PRUs' – although the data is somewhat different for AP free schools, suggesting they may be used more preventatively than post-exclusion. The second group comprises all those covered by the AP census: hospitals (as distinct from hospital schools); independent schools (including independent special schools and independent AP); non-maintained special schools; and other institutions classified as 'not a school'. Many are in fact places where children receive an alternative type of education to state-funded mainstream and special schools, over the long-term. We shall refer to these as 'local authority AP'.

How many children in AP have SEND?

What is initially arresting about the SEND data on AP is that the proportion of children with identified SEND is over five times higher than in the general school population.

The SEND data published by the DfE includes only the 16,134 children sole registered in PRUs. It is harder to find similar data on the 26,128 learners educated in local authority AP.[2] However, given that at least 4000 of these are

2   Even though the AP census does collect that data, it is not included in the DfE's published SEN statistics or the AP census data release.

in non-maintained special schools, and we cannot be certain about the type of provision offered by the 'independent school' or 'not a school' establishments in this category, sticking to the PRU population may provide a clearer picture of what we typically conceive as AP, in any case (FFT Education Datalab, 2017).

Of these 16,134 children, 81% have SEND, compared to 14.9% in the general school population (including AP and special schools); and 13.4% have an EHCP, compared to 3.1% in the school population – a ratio of about 4:1. SEN Support accounts for 67.6% of all children in AP, compared to 11.9% in the school population, which is a ratio closer to 6:1. It's not surprising that the ratio for EHCP would be lower than that for SEN Support, as some children with an EHCP will be educated in special schools, whereas this is generally not an option for children on SEN Support. What might seem surprising, however, is that the proportion of children in AP with an EHCP should still be so high.

The placement figures can help put this in some perspective. Of all children in England with an EHCP, just 0.8% are placed in AP, while 43.8% are in state-funded special schools, 47.9% in mainstream and 6.1% in independent schools. Of all children with SEN support, 1.0% are placed in AP, 91.1% are in mainstream, 7.1% in independent provision and 0.2% in state-funded special schools.

How do learners end up in AP?

Exclusion from school is not the only route into AP. In fact, only 45% of children enter state-funded AP via the official exclusion route (FFT Education Datalab, 2019). For AP free schools, this figure is much lower, at 13%. The school census does not collect data on the reasons why learners are in AP, so we do not know this information for the other 55%. For those in local authority AP, this data is now gathered, and includes categories such as 'mental health need', 'pregnancy/ childcare', 'setting named on an EHCP', and 'physical health need'. It would be useful to have this data for all children in AP.

While there is no way of viewing the SEND status of all learners on entry to AP, we can look at the SEND status of learners at the point of exclusion. Of the 7720 children permanently excluded in 2016-17, 3605 (46.7%) had an identified SEND (DfE, 2018).

The rate of permanent exclusion (from mainstream and special schools combined) for children with SEN Support is 0.35%, and for children with an EHCP, 0.16%, compared to 0.06% for learners with no SEND. In secondary schools, where most of the exclusions occur (6385), permanent exclusion rates are 0.67% for SEN Support and 0.31% for children with an EHCP, compared to 0.14% for those with no SEND.

Looking at the primary area of need, the highest rate by a long way is for children with social, emotional and mental health needs (SEMH) as their primary need (1.09% of all children with SEMH), who accounted for 26.3% of all permanent exclusions in 2016-17 (2030 learners). The next highest rates are 'other difficulty/ disability', 'no specialist assessment' and specific learning difficulty (SpLD) each accounting for less than half a % of all permanent exclusions.

The Timpson Review of exclusions (2019) took these rates and adjusted for other factors, to see whether other forms of disadvantage could account for the large differences. Overall, it revealed that having an EHCP can sometimes be a protective factor against permanent exclusion but that after controls, children with SEN Support were still more likely than their peers to be permanently excluded. Timpson proposes two hypotheses to explain the protective effect of an EHCP: either because the support these children receive makes it less likely they will behave in a way that leads to a permanent exclusion, or because of the guidance, which says that headteachers should 'as far as possible' avoid excluding children with an EHCP. Learners with EHCPs were still more likely to receive a fixed-term exclusion than those with no SEND.

The report also revealed a nuanced picture about the likelihood of exclusion by type of SEND. Children receiving SEN Support for autism, sensory impairment or physical difficulty were no more or less likely to be permanently excluded than their peers, after controlling for other factors. Those with an EHCP for one of these primary needs were significantly less likely to be permanently excluded.

For those with SEMH as a primary need, however, there's a very different picture. After controls, children receiving SEN Support were still 3.8 times more likely to receive a permanent exclusion. Interestingly, however, those with an EHCP for SEMH were no more or less likely to be permanently excluded than their peers without SEND.

Other types of need that are associated with a significantly higher chance of permanent exclusion are behavioural, emotional and social difficulties (an outdated category that was partially replaced in 2014 by SEMH), moderate learning difficulty (MLD), SpLD, and the catch-all categories of 'no specialist assessment', 'other difficulty/disability' and 'SEN type not recorded'.

Interestingly, while having an EHCP seems to be a protective factor in terms of exclusion, the same cannot be said about the likelihood for these learners of receiving their full-time education in AP. While children with EHCPs account for 4.8% of permanent exclusions, they make up 13.4% of learners sole registered in AP (compared to 1.6% for primary schools and 1.7% for secondary schools).

Why is the SEND rate higher in AP than for excluded learners?

There are several possible explanations for the fact that 81.0% of children in AP have an identified SEND, but only 46.7% of excluded children.

First, APs might be better than mainstream schools at assessing for SEND. There is no legal requirement for APs to screen for SEND on entry, but it is reasonable to assume they are doing this at a higher rate than mainstream. (This of course raises the question of whether better assessments in mainstream could help prevent children getting to the point of exclusion.)

Second, children entering AP via routes other than permanent exclusion might have a much higher rate of SEND than excluded children. Alternative routes into AP include managed moves, pregnancy, and moving into the country or local authority area mid-year. While we do not have data to test this hypothesis, there would seem to be no reasonable explanation as to why these children would have such a high proportion of SEND that they would be responsible for almost doubling the rate.

Third, as cited above, we know that 52% of LAs are using AP (at least to some extent) due to a lack of other specialist provision (Isos Partnership, 2018). While we do not have figures for how many learners this affects, it is reasonable to assume that this occurs less commonly in PRUs, and more in the kind of provision that falls into the AP census – which lists 4000 learners in non-maintained special schools, and 12,400 in 'independent school/AP' (FFT Education Datalab, 2017).

Fourth, children might be developing SEND after being placed in AP. The rate of increase is highest for SEMH: only 26% of excluded children have identified SEMH, but 64% of children in AP – representing a 147% increase.

While this may be partly attributed to identification of need post-exclusion, there is also evidence that exclusion can worsen children's mental health. Research conducted by the Child and Adolescent Psychiatry team at the University of Exeter's medical school in 2017 detected a bi-directional association between psychological distress and exclusion – meaning that not only were children with poor mental health more likely to be excluded, but children who had been excluded were more likely to have developed a mental health disorder three years later (Ford et al., 2018).

Social, emotional and mental health needs

Of the 81% of children in AP with a recorded SEND, the largest category of primary need – by a mile – is social, emotional and mental health. The remainder of this chapter will therefore focus on this area of need.

The Isos Partnership's Market Analysis of AP in 2018 reported:

Another strong theme we heard described during the fieldwork was of pupils who had SEN but whose needs had not been identified in mainstream school or who had been given the label of 'SEMH' when further assessment revealed that pupil's behaviour was the result of underlying and unmet communication and interaction or learning needs.

This observation is supported by a body of research literature linking language and learning with behavioural problems in school-age children. One literature review of 26 studies from 2002 found that 'approximately three out of four children (71%) formally identified with emotional and behavioural disorders (EBD) experienced clinically significant language deficits and approximately one out of two (57%) children with diagnosed language deficits also were identified with EBD' (Benner, 2002).

A more recent meta-analysis of 22 studies (Hollo et al., 2014) looked at 1171 children aged 5-13 with formally identified EBD and no history of developmental, neurological or language disorders. The authors found that prevalence of below-average language performance was 81%, and the mean comprehensive language score was significantly below average. They summarised the evidence thus:

Although causal or directional mechanisms of these relations have yet to be established, descriptive evidence supports a strong association between linguistic and behavioural competence. That is, children who exhibit problem behaviour tend to have low language proficiency, and children with low language proficiency tend to exhibit problem behaviour (ibid.).

The authors recommended language screening for all learners with EBD, more research to clarify the relationship between language and behaviour, and interventions to ameliorate the effects of these dual deficits.

What can be done to support children with SEMH in mainstream schools?

It is all too common to expect schools to remedy all kinds of societal ill that they are not equipped or funded to deal with, and mental health is one of these. Schools should not be responsible for providing the kind of support that children may need to deal with complex family circumstances that are impacting their wellbeing and mental health. Several research reports into school exclusion have emphasised the need for better partnership working between mental health services, local authorities and schools (e.g. DfE 2014, Isos Partnership 2018, DfE 2019). But given that schools are the place that most children attend, they often end up having to deal with the resulting behaviour.

A Commons Health Select Committee inquiry in 2014 concluded that 'there are serious and deeply ingrained problems with the commissioning and provision of children's and adolescents' mental health services.' They reported concerns about access to inpatient services; increased waiting times; high referral thresholds; and many Clinical Commissioning Groups (CCGs) reporting that they have frozen or cut their budgets.

The government's 2017 green paper, Transforming Children and Young People's Mental Health Provision, promised one designated senior lead for mental health in every school and college by 2025, mental health support teams working with schools and colleges, and shorter waiting times for young people.

It has followed up these promises with action: the pilot areas for the support teams were announced in early 2019, and in July 2019, the DfE announced the national roll-out of a £9.3 million training scheme. Starting in September 2020, the Link Programme, developed by the Anna Freud Centre, will offer training to up to 22,000 schools and colleges, including alternative provision settings. An independent evaluation of the pilot phase (Day et al., 2017) showed that it was successful in improving joint working and frequency of contact between schools and colleges and mental health services; knowledge and awareness of mental health issues in schools; and quality and consistency of referrals.

Questions have been raised about whether these measures are sufficient. In July 2018, the Education and Health and Social Care select committees conducted a joint inquiry into the green paper and concluded that it 'lacks any ambition and fails to consider how to prevent child and adolescent mental ill health in the first place'. They added that it fails to take several vulnerable groups into account (including looked-after children and excluded children), and that 'the proposals put more pressure on the teaching workforce without sufficient resources'. The report also raised concerns that funding had not been guaranteed, criticised the lack of specific consideration of AP, and recommended that PRUs be equipped with sufficient capacity to meet the mental health needs of their learners.

Researchers from the University of Exeter Medical School who have published work on mental health and exclusions have also warned against the DfE's new drive to invest in early detection of mental health problems if it is not backed up by adequate support. While agreeing that 'efforts to identify and support children who struggle with school may prevent both future exclusion and future psychiatric disorder', they go so far as to call the proposals 'potentially unethical if Child and Adolescent Mental Health Services (CAMHS) or specialist educational needs services lack the capacity to respond and/or school budgets are not allocated to support the recommendations made after specialist assessment' (Ford et al., 2018). They point to previous work which suggests that children whose poor mental health is recognised by parents and/or teachers are more likely to be excluded than those whose psychiatric disorder is not recognised.

Should most AP provision effectively be SEMH specialist schools?

The DfE lists 558 specialist SEMH schools across the country, although availability varies by local authority. Of the 118 local authorities that responded to the Isos Partnership 2018 survey, 88% said they had some form of specialist provision for SEMH. The majority (68%) of places in specialist SEMH are commissioned for secondary-age learners, compared to 32% in primary (although identification of SEMH is increasing at a faster rate in primary than secondary). While the bulk of places in both phases are commissioned from special schools, SEMH units within schools are more common in the primary phase (15% of places) than secondary (4%).

The DfE is investing in more new specialist SEMH schools than AP free schools: in the planned 2020-21 opening of special and AP free schools, only two local authorities were approved for AP schools, while 34 special free schools were approved for 2020-21, of which eight will have an SEMH specialism (Staufenberg, 2017).

Special school places are generally reserved for children with an EHCP, so the question remains over what kind of provision is planned for learners with SEMH SEN Support needs, who do not qualify for an EHCP.

Concluding remarks

There is an ongoing debate about whether the answer to providing for children with SEND is more specialist provision, or better support to include more children with SEND in mainstream schools.

While some children report finding AP much more supportive than mainstream school, there are many ways in which long-term segregation does not prepare children to function in mainstream society – and conversely, children without SEND need to learn how to behave inclusively in a society comprised of people with diverse needs.

But if we are to make schools truly inclusive, we need to invest much more in mainstream. The vision behind the 2014 SEND reforms (DfE, 2015) was to give children the right to a mainstream education, should they choose it. Currently, high-needs funding in mainstream is linked to a particular child's EHCP, with no provision for preventative support for those with SEN Support needs.

The Timpson Review recognised the need for more funds for mainstream schools to work preventatively to support children at risk of exclusion. It is generally assumed that this would come from the existing high-needs budget, but this holds two risks. First, the high-needs budget is already stretched (Staufenberg, 2018) and strong mechanisms will need to be put in place to ensure that this money actually is earmarked for preventative work. It may be necessary to create an additional fund for this purpose. Second, with schools reporting tight budgets (Speck, 2019), mechanisms will be required to ensure that any money allocated to them for preventative work is actually spent on this, rather than absorbed into the main school budget.

Given the high percentage of children with SEND in AP, specialist teachers would seem one good use of any additional funds, along with assessments for SEND for all children identified as at risk of exclusion. Inclusion units may be another. Various schools and trusts run units in which children at risk of exclusion are educated separately within their mainstream school for a short time, where they receive more targeted support and a higher learner-to-teacher ratio. Co-location on the same site as the school means classroom teachers are still available to deliver content, and children can reintegrate into their mainstream classes gradually. The Timpson Review recommended that a 'practice improvement fund' be created, to research and identify best practice in various areas – including how inclusion units are used.

With regards to support for children with SEMH, the government must follow up the ongoing mental health pilots with sufficient investment to roll out successful models across the country. As mentioned by the Exeter research team above, it can be damaging to diagnose mental health needs without putting adequate support in place. We must be careful that the new 'designated teacher' is not expected to be a mental health specialist, merely a link person with professional support services such as CAMHS.

What is clear is that AP should not be a place where learners who cannot function in mainstream are sent to finish their GCSEs, then spewed out into the system to cope alone. More than one in four excluded young people are not in education, employment or training for between one and two years by the time they are 19, compared to one in 10 young people who have never been excluded (DfE, 2011). It is common practice among APs to stay in contact with the learners who leave them, to support their transition process, and FE colleges will often offer transition support. There is no support for transition at system level, however, and this was another of the areas the Timpson Review recommended developing as part of the proposed 'practice improvement fund' for AP. High-needs funding that is available for learners in AP ends brusquely at age 16 for those who have not secured an EHCP by this point. Yet it is naïve to think that any SEMH and learning needs will have been miraculously resolved by the time they finish their GCSEs. There needs to be better long-term support for any learner who has been on the roll of an AP. The government could think of AP as the last chance to identify and provide a support net for a group of young people set to enter adulthood with poor prospects.

All of the above would require additional investment in the high-needs budget – but not more than the lifetime costs of excluded children, which researchers have estimated at £2.1 billion per cohort, in education, health, benefits and criminal justice costs.

References and further reading

Benner, G. J., Nelson, J. R. and Epstein, M. H. (2002) 'Language skills of children with EBD: A literature review.' *Journal of Emotional and Behavioral Disorders*, 10(1): pp. 43–56.

Day, L., Blades, R., Spence, C. and Ronicle, J. (2017) *Mental health services and schools link pilots: Evaluation report*. London: DfE.

DfE. (2011) *Youth cohort study and longitudinal study of young people in England: The activities and experiences of 19 year olds: England 2010*. London: DfE.

DfE. (2014) *School exclusion trial evaluation*. London: DfE.

DfE. (2015) *Special educational needs and disability code of practice: 0 to 25 years*. London: DfE.

DfE. (2018) *Permanent and fixed period exclusions in England: 2016 to 2017*. London: DfE.

DfE. (2019) *Timpson Review of school exclusions*. London: DfE.

FFT Education Datalab. (2017) *Who are the pupils in alternative provision?* Available at: https://ffteducationdatalab.org.uk/2017/10/who-are-the-pupils-in-alternative-provision/ (Accessed: 30 September 2021).

FFT Education Datalab. (2019) *Timpson Review reflections, part one: Not all pupils who end up in alternative provision have been permanently excluded*. Available at: https://ffteducationdatalab.org.uk/2019/05/timpson-review-reflections-part-one-not-all-pupils-who-end-up-in-alternative-provision-have-been-permanently-excluded/ (Accessed: 30 September 2021).

Ford, T., Parker, C., Salim, J., Goodman, R., Logan, S. and Henley, W. (2018) 'The relationship between exclusion from school and mental health: A secondary analysis of the British Child and Adolescent Mental Health Surveys 2004 and 2007.' *Psychological Medicine*, 48(4): pp. 629–641.

Health Select Committee. (2014) *Children's and adolescents' mental health and CAMHS*. London: House of Commons.

Hollo, A., Wehby, J. and Oliver, R. M. (2014) 'Unidentified language deficits in children with emotional and behavioral disorders: A meta-analysis.' *Exceptional Children*, 80(2): pp. 169–186.

House of Commons Education Committee. (2018) *Forgotten children: alternative provision and the scandal of ever increasing exclusions*. London: House of Commons.

IFF Research Ltd. (2018) *Investigative research into alternative provision*. London: DfE.

Isos Partnership. (2018) *Alternative provision market analysis.* London: DfE.

Parker, C., Marlow, R., Kastner, M., May, F., Mitrofan, O., Henley, W. and Ford, T. (2016a) 'The "Supporting Kids, Avoiding Problems" (SKIP) study: relationships between school exclusion, psychopathology, development and attainment – a case control study'. *Journal of Children's Services*, 11(2): pp. 91–110.

Speck, D. (2019) *School funding: £12.6bn needed by 2023, unions say.* Available at: www.tes.com/news/school-funding-ps126bn-needed-2023-unions-say (Accessed: 30 September 2021).

Staufenberg, J. (2017) *Social and emotional needs focus for new SEND schools.* Available at: https://schoolsweek.co.uk/social-and-emotional-needs-focus-for-new-send-schools/ (Accessed: 30 September 2021).

Staufenberg, J. (2018) *Schools to get £350m extra SEND funding, but heads warn it's 'not enough'.* Available at: https://schoolsweek.co.uk/dfe-announces-350-million-for-high-needs-budget-but-critics-warn-its-not-enough/ (Accessed: 30 September 2021).

GLOSSARY OF ABBREVIATIONS

ADHD	Attention deficit hyperactivity disorder
AP	Alternative provision
ASC	Autistic spectrum condition
ASD	Autistic spectrum disorder
CAMHS	Child and Adolescent Mental Health Services
CCG	Clinical Commissioning Group
CIPOLD	Confidential Inquiry into premature deaths of people with learning disabilities
DfE	Department for Education
DISS	Deployment and Impact of Support Staff
EBD	Emotional and behavioural disorders
EEF	Education Endowment Foundation
EHCP	Education, Health and Care Plan
LA	Local Authority
MITA	Maximising the Impact of Teaching Assistants
MLD	Moderate learning difficulty
PMLD	Profound and multiple learning difficulty
PRU	Pupil Referral Unit
SEMH	Social, Emotional and Mental Health
SENCO	Special Educational Needs Coordinator
SEND	Special Educational Needs and Disabilities

SLCN	Speech, language and communications needs
SLD	Severe learning difficulty
SpLD	Specific learning difficulty
SSER	Single-subject experimental research
TA	Teaching assistant